BIOGRAPHICAL SERMON OUTLINES FOR ALL PREACHERS.

Volume 2

(170 Biographical Sermon Outlines on Some New Testament Male and Female Characters)

Important Note:

For some useful information on how to use the eight sermon books for maximum benefit, read the appendix to "A Simple Way to Preach Sermons from the Bible"

STEPHEN ADU-BOAHEN

Contents

PREFACE

Biographical Sermons offer an inexhaustible source of sermons to faithful preachers of God's Word. The Bible contains over 3,000 different male characters. There are also several female characters in both the Old and New Testaments. If we decide to preach only one sermon on each of these 3,000 characters alone (which can never be possible because of the several events in their lives), it will take us not less than 60 years to do this. So if you come into the ministry at 30 years of age, by the time you finish preaching all the biographical sermons alone, you will be over 90 years and will be enjoying your retirement somewhere if the Lord has not already called you home!

So in this brief DISCUSSION, we will want to offer some tit-bits on preaching Biographical Sermons and follow this up with the importance and benefits of preaching such sermons regularly. Biographical Sermons which analyse the lives of Bible characters to learn what positive life lessons they offer us or what negative attitudes we should avoid form one of the numerous sermon types preachers can preach from the Bible.

Apart from offering us numerous sermons to preach on the thousands of characters in the Bible, they are also an effective means of taking the congregation through what most biographical preachers call, "a dramatization of Bible Characters from the pulpit."

It is our firm belief that this book will contribute greatly to your desire as a preacher to preach good and edifying sermons from God's Holy Book. *It is being suggested that you read the introductory*

Preparing and preaching Biographical Sermons on the suggested men and women characters in this book can also go a long way to help us improve upon our preaching. This can help us to vary the Biographical Sermons we can prepare and preach on our own by giving us extra Sermons.

May the good Lord who called us as servants and preachers help us to use this book to preach Bible-based sermons to His flock all the time.

SECTION I
SOME TIT-BITS ON PREACHING
BIOGRAPHICAL SERMONS

Many People Bearing The Same Name

Several people have the same name in the Bible so in preaching sermons on Bible Characters, we must always take time to explain which of these characters we are talking about. Don't leave the congregation to be guessing as to which of the characters is being discussed. Here are a few examples:

- Zechariah - 30 people are mentioned with this name
- Nathan - 20 people are mentioned with this name
- Jonathan - 15 people are mentioned with this name
- Judas - 15 people are mentioned with this name
- Mary - 7 people are mentioned with this name
- James - 5 people are mentioned with this name
- John - 5 people are mentioned with this name

Biographical Sermons are teaching Sermons with Powerful Applications

Romans Chapter 15 verse 4 has this message for the Biographical preacher: "FOR EVERYTHING THAT WAS WRITTEN IN THE PAST WAS WRITTEN TO TEACH US SO THAT THROUGH ENDURANCE AND THE ENCOURAGEMENT OF THE SCRIPTURES WE MIGHT HAVE HOPE."

The Bible story was written around its characters. Therefore it is never possible to study or discuss a Bible event or episode without its characters coming in; neither is it possible to mention or study a Bible character without studying the things he did. If this is the case, then we must see that everything written about the numerous Bible characters and what they did or God used them to do was written to teach us. Some of them suffered, endured, were discouraged, and were afflicted but never gave up. Others were killed and beheaded for their faith; but they stood for God. As we preach Biographical Sermons, we will be teaching all these important spiritual lessons directly from the pulpit. So Biographical Sermons help us to teach useful spiritual lessons! ("Now all these things happened unto them for ensamples: and they are written for our admonition, upon whom the ends of the world are come." 1 Corinthians 10:11) KJV

Biographical Sermons must highlight Positive Character Qualities

Every human being is a human being no matter how high or how low he is in the spirit and in the society. So every character has strengths and weaknesses as well as positive and negative character traits.

If we want to be able to teach precious spiritual lessons with Biographical Sermons, then in every sermon we must bring out and emphasize the positive character qualities in the character being discussed. This will encourage the congregation to think positively that if Brother or Sister so and so met this same problem I am going through and could overcome it by faith, then I can also succeed. The following positive character qualities common to most of the Bible characters are being listed to help you. You can add to it as you study and discover more positive traits in the Bible characters.

1. Intelligent
2. Thoughtful
3. Careful
4. Reasonable
5. Truthful
6. Wise
7. Foresight
8. Imaginative
9. Honest
10. Dependable
11. Loyal
12. Faithful
13. Dedicated
14. Trustworthy
15. Righteous/Holy
16. Obedient
17. Disciplined
18. Strong-willed
19. Persevering
20. Self-controlled
21. Experienced/Mature
22. Good
23. Peaceful
24. Submissive
25. Meditative
26. Prosperous
27. Servant-like
28. Firm
29. Sensitive
30. Contented
31. Cheerful
32. Beautiful
33. Courageous
34. Humble
35. Modest
36. Patient
37. Merciful
38. Loving
39. Gentle
40. Meek
41. Compassionate
42. Kind
43. Zealous

All human beings have their weaknesses. There is no perfect human being on earth. Only the Lord God our omnipotent Father possesses absolute perfection. So in preaching about Bible Characters, we should not try to create the wrong impression that because they excelled and were spiritual heroes in certain areas, they were faultless. The Bible always emphasizes the good side as well as the bad side of all its men and women characters no matter how high God raises them. Examples are Abraham, David, Moses, Peter, the Apostles and several others. So look out for some of the following negative character traits in the Bible Characters and emphasize them as a warning to the congregation to desist from them so that they do not fall into the same traps the characters fell into. The list includes the following: (You can add your own to expand it)

1. Negligent
2. Unreasonable
3. Unbelieving
4. Untruthful
5. Foolish
6. Deceptive
7. Loquacious
8. Weak
9. Impulsive
10. Unfaithful
11. Lying
12. Gossip
13. Lazy
14. Dishonest
15. Rebellious
16. Hypocritical
17. Immoral
18. Fornicator
19. Adulterer
20. Covetous
21. Wasteful
22. Immature
23. Bad
24. Unclean
25. Hasty
26. Contentious
27. Warlike
28. Failure
29. Disobedient
30. Compromiser
31. Poor/Destitute
32. Wicked
33. Sad/Dejected
34. Dull
35. Fearful
36. Indifferent
37. Proud
38. Boastful
39. Self-righteous
40. Presumptuous
41. Sensual
42. Gluttonous/Drunkard
43. Greedy
44. Proud/Arrogant

45. Worldly

SECTION II
ADVANTAGES OF PREACHING BIOGRAPHICAL SERMONS

<u>Biographical Sermons Are More Natural and Practical</u>
Preaching on Bible Characters is more natural and practical than most of the other types of sermons. Whereas other sermon types most of the time offer teaching only, Biographical Sermons not only offer teaching but also the application or misapplication of the teachings and their practical results. As preachers, we could make a great impact by painting these character pictures from the pulpit.

It is the way the Bible handles its characters which makes Biographical Sermons natural and practical and capable of offering us precious lessons and correcting us. In most biographies and autobiographies today, only the best part of the person's character and experience are recorded. Mistakes and failures are either quickly glossed over or omitted altogether. But the Bible always tells the whole story about every man without hiding anything. It paints a person's picture exactly as he is. For instance, it paints Noah as a preacher of righteousness who was very obedient as well as a man of serious excesses. David is mentioned as the man after God's own heart; a loyal King, great soldier, God-fearing man, always seeking God's will, and a great singer. But his adultery and horrible murder are also mentioned.

Abraham is painted as the man of faith who had acted by faith, had left his home country, had believed God's promise, and had received Isaac by faith to become the father of the faithful. But at the same time, his lack of faith in listening to his wife and going into Haggar to give birth to Ishmael is also mentioned. Solomon the wise king, whose sacrifices God received directly with fire, who built a magnificent temple for God, who was mightily blessed by God materially, who wrote many wise sayings and proverbs is also mentioned as failing to live by his own wisdom; marrying several heathen women and backsliding. Balanced lessons from all such Bible Characters make Biographical Sermons very practical and natural to be able to teach and correct us.

Biographical Sermons Make the Bible Lively And Interesting

One great advantage of Biographical Sermons is that whenever they are preached, they make the Bible come alive and awaken a new devotion to it. The preaching is like inviting the characters concerned into the pulpit and asking them to re-enact their stories as they will preach it in personal testimony sermons. Because in their experiences, ups and downs, victories, failures, defeats and so on we also see a reflection of our own lives, it makes such biographical messages very, very personal, interesting and lively!

In working through Israel as a nation and the other Gentile nations to reveal His plan and purpose for the world, God's method was man. Every major event, episode, or activity in the Bible required a man or woman or in some cases both men and women working at the same time to make it happen and become real. This explains why every page of the Bible contains biographies of Bible Characters.

Without Bible characters there could not have been any Holy Bible! When you take Bible Characters out of the Bible you will be left with nothing! Without Moses there would not have been any deliverance in Egypt with all the accompanying miracles; the Exodus, the Law, The Tabernacle and so on. Without Joshua there would not have been any stories of the conquest of the Promised Land. Without the activities of Judges like Gideon, Samson, Ehud, and the rest, there would not have been any Book of the Judges. In the New Testament also, if there were no Jesus, there would not have been any teachings, miracles, healings and parables as we read them in the Gospels today.

In the same way, there would not have been any story of the death, crucifixion, resurrection, and ascension of Christ in the Gospels not to mention important events like the Transfiguration, The Baptism of Jesus, and others. There would not also have been any mention of other characters connected with Jesus' coming and ministry such as John the Baptist, the Apostles, women like Mary Magdalene, the Pharisees, the Sadducees, the Political rulers like Herod, the Gentiles, the Syro-Phoenician woman, the Centurion and many others. But when we read or listen to the stories of these characters as real human beings like us with similar stories like ours to tell, then the Bible no more looks like a book of ancient history but a lively book with lively stories and experiences similar to ours!

ANDREW THE APOSTLE

1

Text: John 1:41

Theme: Precious Lessons from the Life of Apostle Andrew I

INTRODUCTION

Andrew was the first recorded disciple of Christ. His immediate action after coming to Christ as a disciple was to his bring his brother, Simon Peter, also to Jesus. This makes Andrew not only the first disciple of Christ but also the first recorded evangelist in the New Testament. Though he brought his brother Peter to the Lord Jesus Christ, he was often overshadowed by Peter because of Peter's energetic and outspoken nature. In spite of this, there are several good things we can learn from Andrew especially his nature and attitude of always wanting to bring people to Christ. First, he brought his brother, Peter. He also brought the lad with the loaves and fishes which Christ used to perform His great miracle. Again, he brought the Greeks to Jesus when they sought audience with Him. Though Apostle Andrew is not very prominent in the Gospels like his brother Peter, yet he is a character worth studying. His life offers us several useful character qualities which are worth studying and following as we are going to discuss in the first three sermons of this book.

DISCUSSION

I. APOSTLE ANDREW IS A GOOD EXAMPLE OF HUMILITY IN MINISTRY

   1. He responded to Christ's call with Humility. (Matthew 4:18-20)
   2. His call corresponded with Christ's standard of choosing His workers. (1 Corinthians 1:26-29)
   3. If we also want to be true workers and followers of Christ, then we must learn humility from Andrew. (James 4:6, 10)

II. APOSTLE ANDREW IS A GOOD EXAMPLE OF SERIOUSNESS IN MINISTRY

   1. We see this in his leaving everything and immediately responding to God's call. (Matthew 4:20)
   2. By his immediate response to His call, Andrew became enlisted among the chosen disciples of Christ. (Matthew 22:14; Revelation 17:14)

III. ANDREW IS AN EXAMPLE OF THIRST IN MINISTRY

   1. We can never give ourselves to God and work for Him unless we first develop a strong thirst for Him. (Isaiah 55:1, 3)
   2. Apostle Andrew had a strong thirst for God and His work which made him first the disciple of John the Baptist and finally, the disciple of Christ. (John 1:40-41)

IV. APOSTLE ANDREW IS AN EXAMPLE OF HOLY ZEAL IN THE MINISTRY

   1. Christ always calls us into His church and service for a purpose. (Matthew 5:16)
   2. Apostle Andrew exemplified this in bringing his brother, Peter, to Christ who became a useful instrument for Christ. (John 1:41)

V. APOSTLE ANDREW IS AN EXAMPLE OF PROPER VISION IN MINISTRY
   1. Right from the beginning starting from his association with Christ, Andrew understood that Christ had come for the salvation of the whole world. (John 3:16; 14:6; 1 Timothy 2:4)
   2. This understanding showed in his bringing the Greeks to Jesus. (John 12:20-22)

CONCLUSION

Jesus' call, whenever it is extended to us whether for personal salvation or for service in His vineyard always requires good traits and attitudes to make it possible, meaningful and beneficial. This includes all the character attitudes displayed by Apostle Andrew in this sermon such as humility, seriousness, genuine thirst, holy zeal and proper vision. Let us therefore make Apostle Andrew our teacher in these great virtues in this sermon.

2

Text: Matthew 14:18-20

Theme: Precious Lessons from The Life of Apostle Andrew II

INTRODUCTION

The Greek name Andrew which Simon Peter's brother bore means somebody who is strong and manly or somebody who is a great warrior. A manly person is that person who exhibits qualities normally associated with men such as courage, strength and spirit in all his doings. These are qualities which any great warrior also needs to be able to do battles either spiritually or physically or in both situations. Though Andrew is not mentioned in many places in the gospels, we see in the few instances where he is mentioned that he lives up to the meaning of his name such as being the first to brave the storm of criticisms to become the first disciple of Christ, and being bold enough always to bring new people to Jesus. In this sermon, we want to examine more of this manliness as a lesson that once Christ has called us, we must understand that we have become His warriors and that we must fight as courageous soldiers. What other episodes in Andrew's life teach this manliness? They are as follows:

DISCUSSION

I. APOSTLE ANDREW TEACHES US THE NEED TO PRAY
    1. Apostle Andrew was desirous of what the future holds. (Mark 13:4)
    2. This is an attitude which always calls for watchfulness and prayer. (Matthew 26:41; Mark 13:5)

II. APOSTLE ANDREW TEACHES US THE NEED TO SERVE GOD'S PEOPLE
1. Apostle Andrew was very resourceful in the miracle of the feeding of the 5000. (John 6:5-9)
2. Apostle Andrew therefore teaches us the need to be of service to God all the time. (Ecclesiastes 9:10; Romans 12:11)

III. APOSTLE ANDREW TEACHES US THE NEED TO BE PRACTICAL
1. Though Apostle Andrew knew that the two fishes and five small loaves were insufficient in feeding the 5000, he still wanted to be practical to bring this to Jesus to start with. (John 6:5-9 with John 6:10-12)
2. Apostle Andrew's action teaches us that, whenever we become practical and trust God with the little things we have, He is able to do great things with them. (Exodus 14:21; 1 Samuel 17:50)

IV. APOSTLE ANDREW TEACHES US THAT, WE CAN ALWAYS SERVE GOD FAITHFULLY IRRESPECTIVE OF OUR POSITION
1. Though Apostle Andrew was the first disciple of Christ and the bringer of Apostle Peter who together with James and John became the inner circle for Jesus, he did not allow this lack of prominence to deter him from faithful service to Christ. This is another exhibition of his humility. (Romans 12:3)
2. In spite of this lack of prominence, Apostle Andrew did whatever he could for the Lord Jesus. (John 1:41; 6:9; 12:20-22)

V. APOSTLE ANDREW TEACHES US THAT WE MUST BE GOD PLEASERS MORE THAN MEN PLEASERS

1. Even though Andrew was initially the disciple of John the Baptist, who himself told the disciples he was only a forerunner of Jesus (John 1:35-37), when Jesus came, he sought to please God more than men and left John to become the first disciple of Christ (John 1:40).
2. We must learn this great lesson that it is always better to seek to obey and please God rather than men (Acts 5:29)

CONCLUSION

The Lord Jesus always calls us to be of service to Him, to His church and to His people. Though he always calls us to be of service in these ways, He does not want us to forget that we also have a personal salvation to protect through watchfulness, prayer, humility, good manners and proper motives. These are the lessons taught by the life of Apostle Andrew in this sermon. Let us apply them in our lives practically and we shall live and work to see God's glory in the end. Christ has called us because He cares and loves us. To be able to continue to stay in this love, we need the manliness of Apostle Andrew. Let us therefore continue to do everything possible to stay in His love forever through the cultivation of some of the positive virtues discussed in this sermon.

3

Text: Matthew 10:2

Theme: Some important Spiritual Attitudes we can learn from the life of Apostle Andrew in the Church Today I

INTRODUCTION

Positive character traits and attitudes are some of the most important lessons we need to learn from both the Old and the New Testament Saints. The reason is that, salvation does not affect the mind and the heart only but also, the will and our practical lives. This is the reason why Christ emphasizes in John 3:3 that, unless a man is born again, he cannot enter the kingdom of God. This by interpretation means that, unless a man believes and accepts the message of the Gospel after genuine repentance and thereafter allows this message to transform his life and turn him into a brand-new person for Christ, he cannot enter the kingdom of God. Learning precious positive character traits and attitudes from the earlier saints can therefore be of great help in this area. What help does the life of Apostle Andrew offer us in the formation of positive spiritual character qualities to help us in our walk with Christ in the Church today. They include the following which we are going to discuss in two sermons beginning with this first one as follows:

DISCUSSION

I. APOSTLE ANDREW SHOWS US THAT GENUINE SPIRITUAL DESIRE IS ALWAYS IMPORTANT
  1. He became the disciple of both John the Baptist and Jesus because of his intense spiritual desire. (John 1:35-41)

II. APOSTLE ANDREW SHOWS US THAT A TEACHABLE SPIRIT IS IMPERATIVE

   1. He asks Jesus privately about the destruction of the Temple. (Mark 13:3, 4)

III. APOSTLE ANDREW SHOWS US THAT OUR AVAILABILITY IS ALWAYS INDISPENSABLE

   1. When called by Christ, he willingly responded to this. (Matthew 4:18,19; Mark 1:16,17)

IV. APOSTLE ANDREW TEACHES US THE IMPORTANCE OF FAITH

   1. Though knowing it was physically inadequate and impossible to feed five thousand people, he still believed and brought the five loaves and two fishes to Jesus. (John 6:8, 9)

V. APOSTLE ANDREW TEACHES US THE NEED TO BE FRIENDLY

   1. He told Jesus about the Greeks who wanted to see Him. (John 12:20-22)

VI. APOSTLE ANDREW TEACHES US THAT ORDINARY FISHERMEN CAN ALSO BE FAMOUS

   1. He became the first fisherman disciple of Jesus. (John 1:37-40)

   2. He also brought his brother, Peter, another fisherman to Jesus. (John 1:41)

VII. APOSTLE ANDREW TEACHES US THAT SALVATION IS NECESSARY FOR THE WHOLE FAMILY

   1. When he met Christ as the Promised Messiah, he also brought his brother Peter to Him. (John 1:40-41)

CONCLUSION

This sermon and the second one which will follow it are in actual fact a summary outline of the life, call and ministry of Apostle Andrew which is also a perfect pen-portrait of some of the most important spiritual lessons we can learn from any genuine servant of God today. The beauty of the Christian life is that, apart from offering us teachings on all the important things we need to do, it also offers us pictures of genuine servants and men of God who have done this before. When we meet difficulties, we have pictures of men and women who went through similar situations to encourage us. When we meet persecution, we have character pictures of men and women who also met persecution and stood for God to goad us on. Let this character portrait of Apostle Andrew encourage us in all the important areas of the Christian life and ministry into success.

4

Text: Matthew 10:2

Theme: Some important Spiritual Attitudes we can learn from the life of Apostle Andrew in the Church Today II

INTRODUCTION

Positive character traits and attitudes are some of the most important lessons we need to learn from both the Old and the New Testament Saints. The reason is that, salvation does not affect the mind and the heart only but also, the will and our practical lives. This is the reason why Christ emphasizes in John 3:3 that, unless a man is born again, he cannot enter the kingdom of God. This by interpretation means that, unless a man believes and accepts the message of the Gospel after genuine repentance and thereafter allows this message to transform his life and turn him into a brand-new person for Christ, he cannot enter the kingdom of God. Learning precious positive character traits and attitudes from the earlier saints can therefore be of great help in this area. What help does the life of Apostle Andrew offer us in the formation of positive spiritual character qualities to help us in our walk with Christ in the Church today. They include the following which we are going to discuss in two sermons concluding with this second one as follows:

DISCUSSION

I. APOSTLE ANDREW TEACHES US THAT IT IS NECESSARY TO BE GOOD LEARNERS
   1. He became the disciple of John the Baptist to learn from him. (John 1:40)

2. He also became the disciple of the Lord Jesus Christ to learn more from Him. (John 1:37-39)

3. He adopted the attitude of a student to be able to learn more from Jesus. (Mark 13:3,4)

II. APOSTLE ANDREW GIVES US THE LESSON THAT SOMETIMES CHANGE IS NECESSARY IN LEADERSHIP

1. When he walked with John the Baptist for some time and he later saw that Jesus the Messiah Himself had appeared as John the Baptist was always telling his disciples, he did not hesitate to shift to become the disciple of Christ. (John 1:44; John 1:40)

III. APOSTLE ANDREW TEACHES US THE NEED TO PRAY AND WAIT UPON THE LORD

1. He sacrificed everything and met with the disciples to pray after the ascension of Christ. (Mark 16:15; Acts 1:13)

IV. APOSTLE ANDREW TEACHES US THAT WE NEED TO HAVE A GLOBAL OUTLOOK FOR CHRIST

1. As early as the ministry period of Christ, he grew out of the Jewish exclusivity and caught a global vision for ministry by welcoming non-Jews like Greeks to meet Jesus. (John 12:20-22)

V. APOSTLE ANDREW TEACHES US THAT MINISTRY ALWAYS REQUIRES FAITHFUL COMPANIONS

1. He brought Peter to Christ as a companion in ministry. (John 1:40-41)

2. He brought the young boy to Jesus as a companion in the miracle of the feeding of the five thousand. (John 6:8,9)

3. He also met with the other disciples as companions in ministry after the ascension of Christ. (Acts 1:13)

CONCLUSION

This sermon and the previous one which we have already discussed are in actual fact a summary outline of the life, call and ministry of Apostle Andrew which is also a perfect pen-portrait of some of the most important spiritual lessons we can learn from any genuine servant of God today. The beauty of the Christian life is that, apart from offering us teachings on all the important things we need to do, it also offers us pictures of genuine servants and men of God who have done this before. When we meet difficulties, we have pictures of men and women who went through similar situations to encourage us. When we meet persecution, we have character pictures of men and women who also met persecution and stood for God to goad us on. Let these character portraits of Apostle Andrew encourage us in all the important areas of the Christian life and ministry into success.

APOLLOS

1

Text: Acts 18:24

Theme: Good examples from the life and ministry of Apollos

INTRODUCTION

Apollos is another challenging character in the New Testament. Though there is not much information about him, his life presents us with several good examples of the type of character the Lord Jesus Christ needs from His children in His church. Let us look at some of His good examples in this sermon as follows:

DISCUSSION

I. APOLLOS WAS A MAN WHO WAS MIGHTY IN THE SCRIPTURES
   (Acts 18:24)

II. APOLLOS WAS A MAN WHO WAS FERVENT IN SPIRIT
   (Acts 18:25)

III. APOLLOS WAS A MAN WHO WAS BOLD IN SPEECH
   (Acts 18:26a)

IV. APOLLOS WAS A MAN WHO WAS A FORCEFUL SOUL-WINNER (Acts 18:28)

V. APOLLOS WAS A MAN WHO WAS SUBMISSIVE (Acts 18:26b)

VI. APOLLOS WAS A MAN WHO WAS VERY SUPPORTIVE (Acts 18:27)

CONCLUSION

The combination of good characteristics and eloquence with submissiveness such as Apollos possessed and exhibited is rare to find in many people. But Apollos has shown us the way in this sermon that no matter how much the Lord blesses and uses you for His glory in the church you can always be submissive and supportive to bring more glory to His name. How do you measure yourself in this situation in the church in which you find yourself. God is our helper. Amen!

2
Text: Titus 3:13
Theme: Apollos as a Faithful servant of God

INTRODUCTION
Apollos whose name means "Destroyer" walked with the early church workers as a faithful servant of the Lord Jesus Christ. No matter how little our contribution to God's work is in His vineyard, it is always appreciated and honoured by the triune God when done faithfully with a good heart like that of Apollos. Because of the importance of his life lessons to us in this regard, we want to look at the following essential character and ministry qualities about Apollos in this sermon as follows:

DISCUSSION
I. APOLLOS WAS AN ELOQUENT CHRISTIAN (Acts 18:25, 28a)
II. APOLLOS PREACHED AT EPHESUS AND AT CORINTH (Acts 18:24a; 19:1a)
III. FOR GOOD PERSONAL REASONS, APOLLOS REFUSED TO RETURN TO CORINTH
(1 Corinthians 16:12)
IV. APOSTLE PAUL WROTE TO TITUS ABOUT THIS IMPORTANT CHARACTER
(Titus 3:13)

CONCLUSION
If the Church of Christ will forever continue to be both the light and the salt of this world, then, the eloquence and ministry of men like Apollos will always be needed. We always need good

examples like Apollos in the ministry of the Church to help encourage us in faithful and committed service to the Lord Jesus Christ. Our personal gifts must be seen as mere graces to help us eschew pride and arrogance like Apollos exhibited.

BARNABAS

1
Text: Acts 4:36
Theme: Background and Life History of Barnabas

INTRODUCTION
It is always important to study the background and life history of important New Testament Characters like Barnabas. This always throws light on who that character is for us to be able to understand his life story and life lessons. Sometimes, who a person is now is largely dictated by where he is coming from. Let us do this for Barnabas in the following way:

DISCUSSION
I.   BARNABAS HAD AN ENCOURAGING NAME
   1.   His name is an Aramaic name which means "Son of Encouragement." (Acts 4:36-37)
   2.   He lived to fulfil the meaning of his name throughout his ministry and association with people.
II. BARNABAS HAD A GOOD SPIRITUAL NURTURE
   1.   He was a Levite who was born on the Island of Cyprus. (Acts 4:36)
   2.   So, spiritually, he had a good background for ministry. (Acts 11:24a)
III. BARNABAS HAD A GOOD MINISTRY BACKGROUND

1. He was living in Jerusalem at the time the issue of the Greek disciples preaching the Gospel arose. (Acts 11:22)
2. From Jerusalem he went to Tarsus to assist Apostle Paul. (Acts 11:25-26)

IV. BARNABAS PROVIDED A STRONG MINISTRY BACKING

1. He and Paul were responsible for helping to establish the Gospel of free grace at the council in Jerusalem. (Acts 11:22; 14:14)
2. Barnabas and Paul overcame the intense pressure from the Jews on Gentile believers obeying and following the Law before getting salvation. (Acts 15:1, 2)

CONCLUSION

Barnabas had a good name, a good background training as a Levite and a good nature generally which shaped him to become so useful to the church of the Lord Jesus Christ as we see in the New Testament story. A great lesson we can learn from this is summed up in Proverbs 22:6 in the words: *"Teach children how they should live, and they will remember it all their life."* GNT

2

Text: 1 Corinthians 9:6

Theme: Walking in the path of Barnabas as a Christian

INTRODUCTION

Barnabas has a lot of positive character lessons to offer us today. In fact, they are so challenging and so compelling that if we would do our best to cultivate them today, they can help us make a great impact on the church of the Lord Jesus Christ and the work we are doing in it today. He came into the limelight at a very crucial time in the life of the infant church in Jerusalem in its initial missionary endeavours. What are some of these important lessons the life of Barnabas can offer us today. They include the following outlined in the sermon below as follows:

DISCUSSION

I.   BARNABAS LIVED AS A MAN WHO WAS GENEROUS
     (2 Corinthians 9:6; Acts 4:36)

II. BARNABAS LIVED AS A MAN WHOSE CONCERN WAS GENUINE
     (Acts 11:25-30; Hebrews 12:3)

III. BARNABAS WORKED AS A CONCERNED MEDIATOR
     (Acts 9:26-28; Matthew 5:9)

IV. BARNABAS WORKED AS A FAITHFUL MISSIONARY
     (Acts 11:19-23; 13:2; 15:36-40)

V.   BARNABAS LIVED AS A CHRISTIAN WHO WAS SPIRIT-FILLED
     (Acts 11:22-24; Acts 1:8)

VI. BARNABAS LIVED AS A CHRISTIAN WHO WAS SELF-SUPPORTING

(1 Corinthians 9:6, 14)

CONCLUSION

Successful ministry in the Church of the Lord Jesus Christ always depends on two major things. The first one is character, and the second one is contacts. Your character will prove and authenticate you as a genuine messenger of Christ. Your contacts will send you to the place where the task is to be executed. With your good character, strong contacts can easily be established wherever you go to grant you speedy and sure success. Barnabas had both qualities as the facts outlined above in this sermon do show us.

3
Text: Acts 4:36 with Acts 11:23
Theme: Interesting Insights into the life and ministry of Barnabas
I

INTRODUCTION

People like Barnabas are always brought into the church by the Holy Spirit at the right time to further and advance the gospel. Before Barnabas appeared on the scene, the persecution of the infant church was rife and unparalleled. Stephen and Apostle James had been killed and the church members were threatened on all fronts. Barnabas was brought in by the Holy Spirit at this time to bring consolation and encouragement. What are some of the insights we can gain from the life of Barnabas to help us in our lives and ministries today. There are several of them including the following we are going to discuss in the next two sermons as follows:

DISCUSSION

I.   BARNABAS HAD TWO SIGNIFICANT NAMES
1.   At birth, Barnabas was given the name "Joseph" which means "may God add." (Acts 4:36)
2.   The name Barnabas which means "Son of encouragement" or "Son of Exhortation" was later given to him by the Apostles. (Acts 4:36)

II. BARNABAS HAD A GOOD NATIONALITY
1.   Barnabas was a Levite who lived in Cyprus. (Acts 4:36a)
2.   Barnabas was possibly born to some of the Jews in dispersion.

III. BARNABAS HAD A GOOD PRACTICAL NATURE

1. Barnabas was kind and generous as well as openhanded towards material blessings. (Acts 4:37)
2. When everybody was afraid to associate with Paul after his conversion, Barnabas took the risk. (Acts 9:26-27, 28)

IV. BARNABAS HAD AN EXCELLENT SPIRITUAL NATURE
1. Barnabas possessed good spiritual qualities because he was under the full control of the Holy Spirit. (Acts 11:22, 24)
2. Barnabas was a good encourager in the Christian faith at Antioch. (Acts 11:23)

CONCLUSION

As believers under the present dispensation of grace which also happens to be the end-time period with all its evils, backslidings and inordinate lusts for instant wealth and material things, the life of Barnabas can be a good guide for us both practically and spiritually. Though he also met several challenges in his Christian life and ministry, he always did his best to be what he should be and to do what he should do for Christ without wavering. Truly, he is a challenging character!

4

Text: Acts 11:25-26

Theme: Interesting Insights into the life and ministry of Barnabas II

INTRODUCTION

Barnabas was one person who became very useful and very helpful to the early church right from its beginning in Jerusalem until its spread to all parts of the Roman Empire. So, in this sermon, we are going to call him "an asset to the church" and discuss some of the practical and helpful ways in which he became such a great asset to the early church. Whenever Christ gives us the grace to be saved, delivered and freed from the power of Satan like Barnabas, it is mainly to be of service to Him and His righteous Kingdom. How did Barnabas work to become an asset to the church. Let us discuss an aspect of this in this sermon.

DISCUSSION

I. BARNABAS WAS A GREAT ASSET TO THE CHURCH IN MINISTRY
   (Acts 11:25-26, 27-30)
II. BARNABAS WAS A GREAT ASSET TO THE CHURCH IN MISSIONS
   (Acts 13:1)
III. BARNABAS WAS A GREAT ASSET TO THE CHURCH IN THE MEDITERRANEAN
   (Acts 13:4; 14:20) (Acts 14:26-27)
IV. BARNABAS WAS A GREAT ASSET TO THE CHURCH IN PRACTICAL MAINTENANCE

(1 Corinthians 9:6, 12, 18)

CONCLUSION

After going through this sermon, are we mistaken in claiming that Barnabas was a great asset to the church in many ways? Not at all! This sermon has given us the practical proof of this in his practical ministry and support. What title are we also working to gain where we are at the moment in the body of Christ. Is it one which will bring honour and glory to the Lord Jesus or failure and disgrace to His name? Let the good examples of Barnabas be a challenge to us.

5

Text: Acts 15:1-3

Theme: Barnabas the co-apostle to the Gentiles

INTRODUCTION

One of the greatest contributions of Barnabas to New Testament Christianity is his role in helping to bring the gospel of free salvation by grace through faith in the Lord Jesus Christ to the Gentile world. Perhaps it was in preparation for this ministry that God caused him to be born and bred among gentiles on the Island of Cyprus. So when the opportunity came for him to be saved in the early church, he still had his gentile background and nurtured his Gentile sympathies to be used as a co-worker of Apostle Paul to bring the Gospel of Free Grace to all Gentiles. Let us look at how God used him as a great instrument in this ministry in this sermon. The facts are as follows:

DISCUSSION

I. BARNABAS ENCOURAGED PAUL AS THE CHOSEN APOSTLE TO THE GENTILES

   1. Fourteen years after Paul's conversion, Barnabas, along with Titus, accompanied Paul to Jerusalem to secure the acceptance of the other apostles in the holy city for the gospel of grace proclaimed to non-Jews. (Galatians 2:1)

   2. During a private meeting, the leaders of the congregation in Jerusalem affirmed the message the evangelists preached at the church in Antioch. (Acts 15:2-11; Galatians 2:1)

II. BARNABAS WORKED WITH PAUL AS A CO-APOSTLE TO THE GENTILES

1. On one occasion, Barnabas and Peter were led astray by some Jews who claimed that faith was not enough for salvation. (Galatians 2:11-13)

2. As a result, Peter was among the first persons who openly refused to eat with Gentile Christians. (Galatians 2:12)

3. In response, Paul publicly rebuked Peter for his action. Undoubtedly, Paul hoped that by doing so, he could change the minds of others too, including his former mentor, Barnabas. (Galatians 2:14-16)

4. Again, when some Jews came from Jerusalem to claim obedience to the Law before salvation in Antioch in Syria, Barnabas, along with Paul, vigorously opposed them. (Acts 15:1, 2)

5. These two missionaries had witnessed the Spirit at work among Gentiles and lives changed in ways the Mosaic Law could never have accomplished. (Acts 15:12)

6. Barnabas and Paul joined a delegation of believers sent by the church at Syrian Antioch to Jerusalem to deliberate on the matter with the apostles and elders there. Along the way, the entourage told Christians about the conversions of Gentiles in Antioch, along with the places Barnabas and Paul had visited. (Acts 15:2-3)

III. TOGETHER WITH PAUL, BARNABAS SECURED SALVATION BY GRACE FOR THEIR MISSION TO THE GENTILES

1. The Jerusalem church and its leaders welcomed Barnabas, Paul, and the rest of the delegation from Antioch in Syria. (Acts 15:4)

2. At the Council meeting that followed this, Barnabas and Paul described how God had showed His acceptance of

uncircumcised believing Gentiles by enabling the missionaries to perform many signs and wonders among them. (Acts 15:12)

3. As proof, the evangelists mentioned the blinding of a sorcerer on Cyprus, the healing of a crippled man in Lystra, and the large numbers which came to the Lord in Antioch in Pisidia, Iconium, Lystra, and Derbe. (Acts 13:8-12; 14:8-10; 13:43; 14:20-23)

4. At the conclusion of the Council, Barnabas, as well as Paul, Judas Barsabbas and Silas, carried a letter from the Jerusalem church to the congregation at Syrian Antioch. The letter apologized for the disturbance created by the legalists, discredited them, affirmed the integrity of Barnabas and Paul, explained why Judas and Silas had come to Antioch, and asked the Gentile Christians to avoid some behaviours offensive to Jewish believers. (Acts 15:22-29)

IV. THROUGHOUT HIS LIFE, BARNABAS WORKED AS A TRUE CO-APOSTLE TO THE GENTILES

1. Barnabas and Paul had a sharp disagreement on the issue of whether to take John Mark (the cousin of Barnabas) with them or not. (Colossians 4:10; Acts 15:36-39)

2. The reason was that, during the first missionary journey, as the group began to evangelize in Perga, John Mark abandoned the team and returned to Jerusalem. (Acts 13:5, 13)

3. But Paul still not trusting John Mark parted company with Barnabas. (Acts 15:38)

4. Following this, while Barnabas returned to Cyprus with John Mark, Paul took Silas with him to evangelize in Galatia. (Acts 15:39b-40)
5. Barnabas was not only a prophet and a teacher but also a prophet to the Gentiles. (Acts 13:1; 11:24)
6. Tradition says that Barnabas was martyred for his faith in Cyprus.
7. Barnabas' ministry in the early church will forever be remembered for securing freedom to be saved without obeying the law for gentiles and for his altruistic service.

CONCLUSION

If today, all gentiles have the right to seek and obtain salvation by grace through faith in the Lord Jesus, then this was because men like Barnabas and Paul took up the ministry of salvation to non-Jews all over the world. Barnabas will forever be remembered for this feat in ministry. He will also be remembered forever for his desire to perform selfless service to others even when this involved personal suffering.

6

Text: Acts 11:22-24

Theme: The Unique Practical and Ministry Characteristics of Barnabas

INTRODUCTION

Barnabas was a Christian and a worker who was multi-faceted in all his attitudes and behaviour patterns. It was no wonder that he was so versatile in his ministry in different situations as well as in his relationships with different people. This led him to develop a strong character coupled with strong principles on all important matters and issues of ministry. In this sermon, we want to discuss some of these unique and important characteristics to help us function effectively in the church of the Lord Jesus Christ wherever we find ourselves. Some of the details of these important characteristics can be presented in this sermon as follows:

DISCUSSION

I. BARNABAS EXHIBITED THESE CHARACTERISTICS IN HIS PERSONAL MINISTRY (Acts 11:22-23)

II. BARNABAS EXHIBITED THESE CHARACTERISTICS IN HIS JOINT MINISTRY
(Acts 14:1)

III. BARNABAS EXHIBITED THESE CHARACTERISTICS IN HIS DEALINGS WITH MANY MEN (1 Corinthians 9:6; Acts 9:26-27)

IV. BARNABAS EXHIBITED THESE CHARACTERISTICS TO PROVE THAT HE WAS A GENUINE MESSENGER (Acts 11:24)

CONCLUSION

The Church of the Lord Jesus Christ needs more men like Barnabas who can work with different people in different situations at all times. Because the work of the church is a global ministry targeting all human beings everywhere in the world, it further requires workers like Barnabas who can minister to different people with a high level of enthusiasm and commitment. Will you be one of the men like Barnabas? Let us pray for God's grace.

7

Text: Acts 13:1

Theme: Cultivating the Barnabas concepts of ministry today

INTRODUCTION

The way you see ministry determines what you put into it. If your concept of ministry is to please Jesus, this will determine what you will do practically in your ministry. If your concept of ministry is to do everything including sacrificing to bring salvation to the lost, this will also determine the extent you can go in your practical ministry. Whatever Barnabas did in ministry which has brought him credit as a worthy co-apostle of Paul was dictated by the way he understood and gave himself totally to ministry. Let us look at some of these concepts of Barnabas in this sermon to see how they can help us to do more than what we are currently doing for Christ. Some of these concepts can be discussed as follows:

DISCUSSION

I. BARNABAS UNDERSTOOD THAT MINISTRY WAS NOT ABOUT POSITION OR PROMINENCE

1. He accepted and worked under Apostle Paul as a co-worker. (Acts 13:2b-4)

II. BARNABAS UNDERSTOOD THAT MINISTRY WENT BEYOND PREACHING

1. This is seen in Barnabas organising aid for the Jerusalem Church and selling his possessions for the common good of the disciples of the early church. (Acts 4:36-37)

III. BARNABAS UNDERSTOOD TRUE MINISTRY WENT
BEYOND ONLY MEETING THE TEMPORAL NEEDS OF
PEOPLE
1. This is the reason why Barnabas ministered as an Apostle,
Prophet and Teacher. (Acts 13:1)

IV. BARNABAS UNDERSTOOD THAT THE SPREADING OF
THE GOSPEL DEPENDED GREATLY ON PRAYER (Acts
13:2a)

V. BARNABAS BELIEVED THAT SUPPORT IN MINISTRY
COULD BE PERSONAL
(Acts 15:36-39)

VI. BARNABAS WAS A TOLERANT AND A FORGIVING
PERSONALITY (Acts 9:1, 26-27)

VII. BARNABAS UNDERSTOOD AND EXERCISED HIS
THREE-FOLD MINISTRY AS AN APOSTLE, TEACHER
AND PROPHET (Acts 13:1)

CONCLUSION

To be able to do more for Christ in ministry to win His favour
and approval, we must always begin with the right concepts of
ministry which are acceptable by the Lord Jesus Christ as the
head of the Church and are also normal to the ministry ethics of
the Church. This can always ensure our success and lead to
excellence in ministry which will in turn bring fruitfulness and
fulfilment. Whatever we gain from the ministry materially at the
present time, we must understand that our main reward for
service in God's vineyard is in the future when we appear in the
presence of our God in the Bema Judgement after the rapture.

CORNELIUS

1

Text: Jeremiah 29:13

Theme: Cornelius, the Good Man

INTRODUCTION

Cornelius was a man who lived to fulfil what God says in Jeremiah 29:13 in the words: *"And you will seek Me and find Me, when you search for Me with all your heart."* NKJV. Cornelius searched for God with all his heart and when God saw that he was genuine in seeking Him, He gave him the grace to find Him. This is a perfect picture of the true mind and heart with which we must also seek God today. We all need God in our lives but God will never draw close to us until He sees a genuine yearning in our hearts. Cornelius has shown us the way in this sermon with the following details:

DISCUSSION

I. CORNELIUS WAS A MAN WHO FEARED GOD
   1. Cornelius was a centurion. (Acts 10:1)
   2. He truly feared God. (Acts 10:2a)
II. CORNELIUS GAVE PRACTICAL PROOF THAT HE FEARED GOD
   1. His household was also devoted to God. (Acts 10:2a)
   2. Cornelius gave alms to many people. (Acts 10:2b)

3. Cornelius was a man of prayer. (Acts 10:2b; Acts 10:4)

III. CORNELIUS WAS A MAN WHO WAS GOOD

1. Cornelius was a just man. (Acts 10:22b)
2. He received a vision from an angel of God. (Acts 10:3-6, 22c)
3. Cornelius and his household were baptized with the Holy Spirit, just as the apostles had been on the day of Pentecost! (Acts 10:44-45; 11:15)

CONCLUSION

It is not common to have people with the reputation and standing of Cornelius to seek and follow God the way Cornelius did. Many of such people are full of pride and arrogance and walk defiantly before God. But Cornelius was not like that. When God saw that his heart was yearning for Him, He caused His servant Peter to visit him in his home to show him the way of salvation. Thereafter, He baptized him and his household with the Holy Spirit. This is a big spiritual challenge to all of us today.

2

Text: Ephesians 2:8-9

Theme: Cornelius, An example of God's Grace in Salvation

INTRODUCTION

As good as they were, Cornelius and his household still did not know God's way of salvation (Acts 11:14). They needed teaching and instruction on this and when God gave them the grace to get this through Apostle Peter, they gleefully and enthusiastically grabbed this opportunity which was confirmed by God with a mighty baptism with the Holy Spirit. For a Gentile soldier and his household to receive this visitation at a time like this was a demonstration of God's grace and salvation as we learn from this sermon. God wanted more from them, and they stood ready to obey.

DISCUSSION

I. CORNELIUS AND HIS HOUSEHOLD NEEDED TO REPENT TO GET GOD'S SALVATION
   1. Repentance is an important requirement for God's free salvation. (Acts 3:19) (Acts 11:17-18)
II. CORNELIUS NEEDED TO BE BAPTIZED AFTER HIS SALVATION (Acts 10:47-48)
III. CORNELIUS AND HIS HOUSEHOLD NEEDED TO BELIEVE IN CHRIST TO GET GOD'S FREE SALVATION
   1. Faith in Christ is a necessary requirement for obtaining God's free salvation. (John 3:16; 1 John 5:11-13)
IV. CORNELIUS AND HIS HOUSEHOLD HAD TO GIVE PRACTICAL PROOF OF GOD'S SALVATION

1. It is after obtaining God's free salvation that practical
   good works become useful. (Acts 10:48b)
2. If from our hearts we want to be saved like Cornelius, we
   can also try to be good persons like him, practise good
   works and show genuine zeal for this and God will have
   mercy on us. (Acts 10:1-2)

CONCLUSION

The Bible has made salvation accessible to all men everywhere
with the statement: *"For whoever shall call upon the name of the Lord
shall be saved."* NKJV Romans 10:13. But we cannot call upon the
name of the Lord in the right way and in the right manner until
sometimes a messenger of God shows us the way. This was what
exactly happened to Cornelius and his household. When Apostle
Peter showed them the road to God's salvation through faith in
Christ and they took God's word, this opened a great door of
salvation to them. We also have the same opportunity they had.
Are we going to take advantage of it as they did?

3

Text: Matthew 5:6

Theme: The Good Spiritual Characteristics of Cornelius

INTRODUCTION

The name Cornelius means "A Horn" which is a symbol of strength, power, influence and success in the Bible. With this great name, his horn surely had to be lifted before passing out of this world. But what is the main lesson that we must draw from the life of this 'good Soldier' in this sermon? It is that, whenever God sees in our hearts a sincere desire and a hunger for Him, He will also do everything possible to meet it. Let us see how He did this in the life of Cornelius and his household.

DISCUSSION

I.   CORNELIUS WAS A DEVOTED SOLDIER OF THE ROMAN EMPEROR (Acts 10:1)

II. CORNELIUS WAS A DEVOTED ENQUIRER
     (Acts 10:2) (Acts 10:4 Psalm 119:2)

III. CORNELIUS HAD AN ANGELIC ENCOUNTER
     (Acts 10:3-7) (Isaiah 11:3-4)

IV. CORNELIUS WAS AN OBEDIENT MAN
     (Acts 5:29) (Acts 10:3-8)

V.   CORNELIUS WAS A JUST MAN
     (Acts 10:22) (Colossians 4:1)

VI. CORNELIUS HAD A HUMBLE SPIRIT
     (Acts 10:25-27) (Matthew 18:4)

VII. CORNELIUS WAS AN EARNEST SEEKER
     (Acts 10:30-33, 34-35) (Ephesians 5:18)

CONCLUSION

When in Jesus' teaching, He referred to those who hunger and thirst for righteousness, what did He exactly mean? Was Cornelius' life not an example of those who hunger and thirst after righteousness? And what did God promise those who hunger and thirst after righteousness this way? If Cornelius received divine intervention, angelic visitation and a special visit by Peter, a great Apostle, then he deserved these by the intense spiritual hunger and thirst in him to seek and find God. Should this not be a big challenge to us in contemporary Christianity? It should!

EPAPHRAS

1

Text: Colossians 1:7

Theme: Epaphras in the ministry of Christ

INTRODUCTION

Epaphroditus is another character whose brief appearance in the New Testament is very significant as a role model in beginning with the Lord in salvation, sitting at His feet to grow, receiving training in ministry and practically getting involved in the ministry. His life presents us with some of the following important facts which we are going to discuss in this sermon as follows:

DISCUSSION

I. EPAPHRAS CAN GENERALLY BE A GOOD ROLE MODEL IN SEVERAL MATTERS
    1. Epaphras had his origins and hometown as Epaphras' ethnicity and hometown.
    2. Epaphras understood God's way of Salvation. (Romans 3:23) (Ephesians 2:8, 9) (Colossians 1:6)
    3. Epaphras had a good Relationship with Christ. (Colossians 1:7; 4:12a) (Philemon 23)

II. PRACTICALLY, EPAPHRAS CAN BE A VERY GOOD ROLE MODEL IN MINISTRY

1. Epaphras took time to receive Training in the ministry. (2 Timothy 2:2) (Colossians 1:7)
2. Thereafter, Epaphras Exercised His Spiritual Gift as an Evangelist to Plant Churches in the Lycus Valley. (Colossians 1:5-6; 2 Timothy 4:5) (Ephesians 4:11; Colossians 4:12a)
3. Epaphras Conferred with Apostle Paul on some of the Problems in the churches of Lycus Valley. (Colossians 4:13)
4. Epaphras also resorted to prayer Concerning the Problems of the Churches in the Lycus Valley. (Luke 18:1) (Colossians 4:12b; Romans 8:27)

CONCLUSION

It is clear that Epaphras does not return with Tychicus and Philemon when they took the letters to the Lycus Valley. What happened to him after this event, we do not know. Did he stay with Paul in Rome? Was he eventually martyred? Did he return to the Lycus Valley after Paul was released from his imprisonment in Rome? Scripture and church history are silent on these questions. But at least, the three important lessons from his life are clear.

2

Text: Colossians 1:7

Theme: Precious Lessons from Epaphras

INTRODUCTION

When we consider Epaphras among the workers of the New Testament, he can highly be rated for some of the good things he did in some of the churches and what he also did practically in missions and church planting. Let us look at the facts on some of his achievements in this sermon.

DISCUSSION

I. EPAPHRAS WAS A FAITHUFUL MESSENGER (Colossians 1:7)

II. EPAPHRAS WAS A FAITHFUL MINISTER (Colossians 1:7) (1 Timothy 1:12; 2 Timothy 2:2)

III. EPAPHRAS WAS A TRUE MISSIONARY (Colossians 4:13)

IV. EPAPHRAS WAS A MAN OF PURPOSE (Colossians 1:7-8; James 1:27)

V. EPAPHRAS WAS A MAN OF PRAYER (Colossians 4:12b)

CONCLUSION

The work of the Lord Jesus Christ in the church depends upon character, faithful preaching and devotion to prayer. Christ does not work in the church without His vessels like preachers. His preachers and workers in the church cannot also do His work successfully without relying absolutely upon Him in prayer. Epaphroditus excelled in all these areas as an example to us today on how we should walk and work for Christ. Let his life be an inspiration to all genuine Children of God.

3

Text: Romans 8:22-23

Theme: Some prominent Spiritual Lessons from Epaphras

INTRODUCTION

Among all the good things we can learn from the life of Epaphroditus, there are three of them which stand out and deserve special attention. These can be good examples to us both as ministers and faithful disciples of Christ. What are these essential spiritual qualities? Let us discuss them in this sermon as follows:

DISCUSSION

I. EPAPHRAS WAS A MAN OF PROPER PRIORITIES (Philippians 2:25)
II. EPAPHRAS WAS A MAN OF DEEP PASSION (Philippians 2:26, 29) (Colossians 4:13)
III. EPAPHRAS WAS A MAN WHO WAS ARDENT IN PRAYER (Romans 8:22-23) (Colossians 4:12b)

CONCLUSION

When we set our priorities right, we are always able to choose and do what is best for us and also very helpful to others. When we pray fervently as Epaphras did, we develop a deep passion for Christ and His work which also ultimately leads to practical involvement in the ministry and successful labour in the vineyard of Christ. Let us say bravo to Epaphras for showing us the way and pray for the grace to imitate him.

APOSTLE JAMES

1

Text: Matthew 4:21-22

Theme: Some Important Lessons from the Life of Apostle James

INTRODUCTION

The Lord Jesus Christ never made a mistake in calling all the disciples who later became His Apostles. Because in the end we see that each of them had some characteristics which contributed positively to Christ's ministry and mission and to the overall redemptive plan of God. One of these disciples was Apostle James who was called into the inner circle of Jesus throughout His ministry. Both the positive and negative characteristics of Apostle James are going to be discussed in this sermon as follows:

DISCUSSION

I.   APOSTLE JAMES' CONVERSION WAS DRAMATIC
     (Matthew 4:21-22)

II. APOSTLE JAMES' CONVERSION CAME THROUGH DETERMINATION
     (Matthew 4:21-22; 10:37; **Acts 5:29**)

III. APOSTLE JAMES' LIFE WAS CHARACTERIZED BY THUNDEROUS DEVOTION
     (Mark 3:17; Luke 9:54, 55) (Matthew 10:5-6)

IV. APOSTLE JAMES' LIFE WAS CHARACTERIZED BY MINISTRY DEVOTION

(Mark 1:29; 5:37) (Matthew 17:1; 26:37), (Luke 5:10; Mark 13:3) (Luke 9:54; Matthew 20:20-23; John 21:2)

V. APOSTLE JAMES WAS TAUGHT THAT GREATNESS COMES BY DEDICATION

(Matthew 20:23, 25-28)

CONCLUSION

When everything is said and done, one major proof stands out that Apostle James worked to fulfil the purpose of His call without disappointing the Lord Jesus Christ. From the day of his call to the end of the ministry of Christ and to the gathering of the disciples in the upper room, Apostle James never departed from his master. His ministry continued well after Pentecost until the Lord gloriously called him home. His dedication to Christ can never be forgotten.

2

Text: Luke 6:13, 14 with Acts 12:2
Theme: The story of James the Apostle

INTRODUCTION

Apostle James was another great figure among the disciples who were called by Christ. After Pentecost, he had a great ministry in the early Church because he had humbled himself to be trained by Christ as a disciple. Let us look at a summary of his life in this sermon as follows:

DISCUSSION

I. JAMES WAS CALLED LIKE ALL THE OTHER DISCIPLES
    1. He was called to be an apostle. (Matthew 4:21, 22; 10:2; Mark 1:19, 20; Luke 6:14; Acts 1:13)
    2. He had a surname Boanerges which means son of thunder. (Mark 3:17)
II. JAMES WAS TRAINED LIKE ALL THE OTHER DISCIPLES
    1. He became an intimate companion of Jesus and was with Him at the great draught of fishes. (Luke 5:10)
    2. He was present at the healing of Peter's mother-in-law. (Mark 1:29)
    3. He was present at the raising of the daughter of Jairus. (Mark 5:37; Luke 8:51)
    4. He was present at the transfiguration of the Lord Jesus. (Matthew 17:1; Mark 9:2; Luke 9:28)
    5. He was with Jesus at Gethsemane. (Matthew 26:37; Mark 14:33)

6. He questioned Jesus about His second coming. (Mark 13:3-4)
7. He was present at the Sea of Galilee when Jesus revealed himself to the disciples after His resurrection. (John 21:2)

III. JAMES DIED LIKE MOST OF THE OTHER DISCIPLES

1. James died as a martyr just as tradition says most of the other disciples also died. (Acts 12:2)

CONCLUSION

Apostle James had a fruitful but short ministry as compared to that of the other Apostles. But God always has a separate plan for each and every one of us. In His plan Apostle James had to end his ministry earlier as a martyr probably to fulfil another great ministry spiritually in heaven. Whatever be the case, he was called, consecrated, commissioned, and finally called home. Let us all learn to endure and stand for Christ as he did, for great is our reward in heaven. Amen!

JAMES THE BROTHER OF JESUS

1

Text: Acts 1:14 with 1 Corinthians 15:7
Theme: Meeting James, the brother of Jesus

INTRODUCTION

It is true that God works in mysterious ways to fulfil His plans and purposes for His children. It was the hand of God upon James, the brother of Jesus, which helped him to finish the Christian race successfully. His life story offers us several challenges including the following we are going to discuss in this sermon.

DISCUSSION

I.   THE NAME "JAMES" MEANS A SUPPLANTER
II. JAMES WAS A SIBLING
     (Matthew 13:55; Mark 6:3; Galatians 1:19)
III. JAMES WAS A SKEPTIC
     (John 7:5) (Matthew 13:57)
IV. JAMES LATER BECAME A SUPPORTER
     (Acts 1:14; 1 Corinthians 15:7) (John 3:3)
V.   JAMES FINISHED OFF AS A SHEPHERD
     (Galatians 1:19; Acts 12:17; Hebrews 13:17)
VI. JAMES WORKED FOR CHRIST AS A SCRIBE

(James 1:1)

CONCLUSION

Though James was the half-brother of the Lord Jesus Christ Himself, he almost missed the salvation brought to the world through Jesus. Initially, he was skeptical about the claims of Jesus but thanks be to God that later, he became converted to Christ and worked in the Church. His life offers us a big lesson. It does not matter who you are, God has the same standard of salvation for everyone who comes to Him.

2

Text: Mark 6:3

Theme: Some Important Historical facts about James, the half-brother of Jesus

INTRODUCTION

The Bible makes us aware that after the birth of Jesus by the virgin Mary, Mary cohabited with her husband Joseph in a normal marital relationship and gave birth to other children including this James we are going to discuss in this sermon. The story of Jesus' siblings in the Gospels is very interesting. In that, it reminds us of the truth that in the matter of salvation, God is no respecter of persons. All men are expected to meet the requirements of salvation through repentance, faith in Christ and genuine conversion leading to New Life. Let us look at the life of James in this sermon as it conforms to these and other important standards of God.

DISCUSSION

I. JAMES WAS TRULY THE BROTHER OF JESUS (Mark. 6:3; Galatians 1:19)

II. INITIALLY, JAMES WAS NOT A BELIEVER IN JESUS (Mark 3:21; John 7:3-5)

III. AFTER CHRIST'S RESURRECTION, JAMES CHANGED TO BELIEVE IN JESUS(1 Corinthians 15:7)

IV. JAMES ENDORSED PAUL'S GOSPEL ABOUT JESUS (Galatians 2:9; Romans 10:9-13)

V. IT IS LIKELY AFTER THEIR CONVERSION, JAMES AND HIS BROTHERS PREACHED ABOUT JESUS (1 Corinthians 9:5)

CONCLUSION

According to Josephus, the Jewish historian who lived around the time of Christ and wrote to confirm all the facts discussed above about James, James was killed by the Jewish leaders for being a breaker of the Law of Moses. They opposed Jesus and all His true followers like James. So it is no wonder they planned his death like his senior brother Jesus whom they killed by accusing Him of making Himself equal to God.

As we looked at earlier, Luke and Paul said that James was a leader in the Jerusalem church. Josephus tells us he was stoned to death in the city. The reason why this is a big deal is while James travelled, his home base was Jerusalem, the very city that Jesus was crucified. If you want to spread a far-out story, you don't do it in the city of the alleged events where you can easily be contradicted. Also, by preaching in the city that his brother was killed in, he would be inviting the same kind of persecution.

JESUS

1

Text: Luke 2:7

Theme: The Story of the Birth of Jesus

INTRODUCTION

The miraculous conception and birth of the Lord Jesus was improbable. But by God's omnipotent power, it became possible. His earthly mother Mary, wondered how this could take place since she knew the only road to conception was through sexual intercourse between a man and a woman. But when Angel Gabriel told her that Jesus' case was different because it was going to be effected by the power of the Holy Spirit, she took it like that, believed it and waited for it. Finally, it came to pass in the manger exactly as Angel Gabriel had predicted. The details are going to be discussed in this sermon as follows:

DISCUSSION

I. JESUS WAS BORN IN A MANGER
    (Luke 2:7)
II. JESUS WAS BORN WITHOUT A MIDWIFE
    (Luke 2:4-7)
III. THE MIRACULOUS BIRTH OF JESUS BROUGHT THE VISIT OF THE MAGGI
    (Matthew 2:1-12)

CONCLUSION

Jesus could live in this sinful world without committing any sin because He was not born with the sin nature we all inherited from Adam and Eve. We inherit the sinful nature when a sinful father goes into a sinful mother and the two of them conceive and bring forth a sinner like them. But Jesus was not born out of a conception which took place after Joseph had met Mary for sex. This way Mary only became a pure vessel to carry the pure baby Jesus whose conception was caused by the pure Holy Spirit to the glory of the pure Father! It is only the creator God who can cause such a thing to happen in our world. Today medical science is causing some women to conceive outside the womb. But the medical doctors still need the living sperm of a man to make this possible. Only Jesus came into the world in a way different from all other persons. Glory be to the name of our living and powerful God!

2

Text: Psalm 40:8

Theme: Pictures of Obedience from the Life of Jesus

INTRODUCTION

Obedience is a virtue which we all need as Christians if we want to finish the Christian race successfully. Unfortunately, the one thing which the devil, our arch-enemy always seeks to promote in our lives is disobedience. Through disobedience Adam and Eve fell in the garden of Eden. Through disobedience Israel saw defeat at Ai. Through disobedience many people turn away from the Lord Jesus Christ and are unable to complete the spiritual journey. What can we learn from the Lord Jesus Christ in this sermon to help us walk in obedience to the Father as He did? To answer this question, let us look at the following pictures of obedience portrayed by Christ in this sermon as follows:

DISCUSSION

I. OBEDIENCE WAS PREDICTED TO HAPPEN (Psalm 40:8; Isaiah 11:5; 50:5, 6; Hebrews 10:7-9)

II. OBEDIENCE WAS MANIFESTED IN HIS EARTHLY HOUSEHOLD
(Luke 2:51)

III. OBEDIENCE WAS MANIFESTED IN HIS HEAVENLY HOME
1) He showed obedience to God. (Luke 2:49; John 4:34; 5:30, 36; 6:38; 8:29, 46, 55; 9:4; 14:31; 15:10; 17:4)
2) He showed obedience in His baptism though He was not a repentant sinner. (Matthew 3:15)

IV. OBEDIENCE HAPPENED TO BRING HOPE

1) It brought hope through his sufferings. (Matthew 26:39, 42; Mark 14:36; Luke 22:42; Hebrews 5:8)
2) It brought hope through his death. (John 19:30; Philippians 2:8)

CONCLUSION

Christ has given us clear pictures of what it means and what it involves to walk in practical obedience before God. First, it must show in how we walk with God Himself. Next, it must show in how we demonstrate it in our earthly home. Thirdly, it must show in altruistic service in the household of God. May the Holy Spirit always help us in this! Amen

3

Text: 1 John 2:6

Theme: Some Practical Lessons We can learn from the Life and Character of Jesus

INTRODUCTION

The Lord Jesus Christ left us great examples of everything we need to know and do as Christians before He went back to the Father after His resurrection. This is why many people have bound themselves with the question, *"What did Christ do or say about this?"* before they do anything as Christians. This is good and accords perfectly well with the statement in the Bible which says that if we claim to be true followers of the Lord Jesus Christ, then with the help of the Holy Spirit, we ought to walk as He also walked. This sermon aims at showing us some of the things Jesus taught us in His practical and ministry life to be copied and followed as Christians. It shows in the following important areas:

DISCUSSION

I. IT SHOWS IN DOING GOD'S WORK

1) By Christ giving himself as a sacrifice. (Luke 9:51; 12:50; 13:32, 33; 1 Timothy 6:13)

2) By Christ, showing zeal for God's house. (Luke 2:49; John 2:13-17; Psalm 69:9)

3) By Christ constantly preaching the gospel. (Matthew 4:23; 9:35; Luke 4:43; Mark 1:38)

II. IT SHOWS IN OUR PERSONAL WALK

1) It showed in Christ's total obedience to God. (John 4:32, 34; 9:4; Romans 15:3)

2) It showed in Christ always doing good. (Acts 10:38)

CONCLUSION

Almost all the things we can do in the Church as sincere Christians and followers of Christ can be grouped into two. First, it relates to how we walk as Christians and secondly it relates to how we work for God as Christians. In this sermon, Christ Jesus has shown us some of the things we can do as workers of Christ in accordance with Ephesians 4:11. He has also shown us how we should walk to give credence to the gospel. Let us pray that the Holy Spirit will help us to see these in our lives and ministries.

> <u>Ephesians 4:11</u>
> *And He Himself gave some to be apostles, some prophets, some evangelists, and some pastors and teachers.* NKJV

4

Text: 1 Peter 2:21

Theme: Christ, our Great Mentor

INTRODUCTION

We are in an age in which everybody is talking about mentorship and the need to have mentors. This is a good idea because it is also an effective means of attaining success. But the best mentor we can always add to our numerous mentors is the Lord Jesus Christ Himself. He alone can provide us with the best mentorship both spiritually and physically today. We can get proof of this in this sermon which has the following details:

DISCUSSION

I.   CHRIST IS OUR PERFECT EXAMPLE IN CHARACTER
1) Christ is our example in normal character. (Romans 8:29; 15:2, 3, 5, 7; 1 Peter 1:15, 16; 1 John 3:1-3, 16; 4:17)
2) Christ is our example in meekness. (Matthew 11:29; Hebrews 12:3; 1 Peter 2:21-24)
3) Christ is our example in humility. (Luke 22:26, 27; John 13:13-15; 2 Corinthians 10:1; Philippians 2:5-8)

II. CHRIST IS OUR PERFECT EXAMPLE IN SHOWING CARE AND CONCERN
1) Christ is our best example in loving others. (John 13:34; Ephesians 5:2)
2) Christ is our best example in enduring suffering for God. (1 Peter 3:17, 18)

III. CHRIST IS OUR PERFECT EXAMPLE IN MINISTRY COMMITMENT

1) Christ is our best example in ministering. (Matthew 20:28; Mark 10:43-45; 2 Corinthians 8:9; Galatians 6:2)

CONCLUSION

When you make Jesus your mentor and example as discussed in this sermon, then you have set foot on the sure path to success because His mentorship will shape your character, shape your ministry and work, and also shape your social interactions and inter-personal relationships. These are the major ingredients needed for success by all men and women on earth irrespective of the type of work you are doing. Will you make Jesus your mentor today? Do so because you will have everything to gain and nothing to lose! Amen!

5

Text: 1 John 2:6

Theme: Walking as Christ walked (I)

INTRODUCTION

The Lord Jesus Christ did not only teach us how to be Christians; He also demonstrated how we can walk as Christians in practical terms by His own example so that when we forget His teachings on how we should walk, at least, we will remember the practical aspect of how we should walk to be able to please and glorify the Father. In this and the next sermon which will follow it, let us learn God's spiritual principles on walking with Him successfully as Christians with the following details:

DISCUSSION

I. WE MUST WALK WITH LOVING PASSION
   (John 13:1; John 15:13; 1 Corinthians 13:3)
II. WE MUST WALK WITH JOYFUL POSTURE
   (Proverbs 15:13; John 15:11; John 17:13)
III. WE MUST WALK IN PEACE
   (Matthew 5:9; Colossians 3:15; Philippians 4:7)
IV. WE MUST WALK WITH PATIENCE
   (Matthew 27:14; Romans 12:12; James 1:3,12)
V. WE MUST WALK IN KINDNESS WITH THE SPIRIT OF PHILANTHROPY
   (Ephesians 4:32)

CONCLUSION

There is nothing more important than walking by these virtues which the Lord Jesus Christ Himself demonstrated in His practical life on earth as the Son of Man, with the Holy Spirit being our helper. Though most of these moral virtues are neither existent nor popular in our world today, the Holy Spirit can still guide us to exhibit these truths in our practical lives as true Children of God if we totally rely upon Him as Christians. May He help us to walk as we have discussed in this sermon.

6

Text: 1 John 2:6
Theme: Walking as Christ walked (II)

INTRODUCTION

The Lord Jesus Christ did not only teach us how to be Christians; He also demonstrated how we can walk as Christians in practical terms by His own example so that when we forget His teachings on how we should walk, at least, we will remember the practical aspect of how we should walk to be able to please and glorify the Father. In this second sermon like the previous one discussed, some additional principles on our walking with God successfully can be put together and discussed as follows:

DISCUSSION
I.   WE MUST WALK BY SHOWING GOODNESS
     (Matthew 19:16)
II. WE MUST WALK IN GENTLENESS
     (Isaiah 40:11; Philippians 4:5; 2 Timothy 2:24)
III. WE MUST WALK BY BEING ON OUR GUARD
     (1 Thessalonians 5:22)
IV. WE MUST WALK BY BEING FORGIVING
     (Luke 23:34; Ephesians 4:32; Colossians 3:13)
V.   WE MUST WALK WITH ABSOLUTE FAITHFULNESS
     (Matthew 17:19, 20; 25:21; 1 Corinthians 12:9; Hebrews 11:1; 1 Thessalonians 5:24)

CONCLUSION

There is nothing more important than walking by these virtues which the Lord Jesus Christ Himself demonstrated in His practical life on earth as the Son of Man, with the Holy Spirit being our helper. Though most of these moral virtues are neither existent nor popular in our world today, the Holy Spirit can still guide us to exhibit these truths in our practical lives as true Children of God if we totally rely upon Him as Christians. May He help us to walk as we have discussed in this sermon.

7

Text: 1 John 2:6

Theme: Walking as Christ walked (III)

INTRODUCTION

In our walk with God, because we are living in the world with several people around us, the way we walk and conduct ourselves affects several lives either in business or in normal interpersonal relationships. Jesus has given us all the necessary precepts and examples we need to follow successfully in this and the next sermon as follows:

DISCUSSION

I. WE NEED TO WALK IN HUMILITY
(Luke 22:27; Philippians 2:8; 1 Peter 5:3–5)

II. WE HAVE TO WALK WITH ABSOLUTE HONESTY
(2 Corinthians 8:21; Ephesians 4:25)

III. WE NEED TO WALK WITH FORTITUDE (Deuteronomy 31:6; 1 John 4:4)

IV. WE NEED TO WALK WITH FRATERNITY AND FRIENDSHIP (Proverbs 27:17)

V. WE NEED TO WALK IN FAIRNESS (Matthew 7:12)

CONCLUSION

If we were to allow the Holy Spirit to help us to walk as Jesus walked as discussed in this sermon, would the Church of Christ and even the whole world not be turned into a little paradise. Most Christians know the value of these attributes but societal and economic pressures are forcing them to live contrary to these truths. So what must we also do after learning, discussing and seeing these truths in the practical life of Jesus our Master. Let the Holy Spirit be our help and support in this area also! Amen!

65

8

Text: `1 John 2:6

Theme: Walking as Christ walked (IV)

INTRODUCTION

In our walk with God, because we are living in the world with several people around us, the way we walk and conduct ourselves affects several lives either in business or in normal interpersonal relationships. Jesus has given us all the additional precepts and examples we need to follow to be able to do this successfully in this sermon as follows:

DISCUSSION

I.   WE NEED TO WALK IN GRATITUDE
     (1 Corinthians 4:7; 1 Thessalonians 5: 18)

II. WE NEED TO WALK WITH FULL GENEROSITY
     (Deuteronomy 16:17; Matthew 10:8)

III. WE NEED TO WALK IN CONTENTMENT AND GRATIFICATION
     (Romans 9:19–21; Philippians 4:10–13; 1 Timothy 6:6–9)

IV. WE NEED TO WALK TO BE TOTALLY RELIABLE
     (1 Corinthians 4:2; Colossians 1:10)

V.   WE NEED TO WALK BY BEING FULLY RESPONSIBLE
     (Romans 14:12)

CONCLUSION

If we were to allow the Holy Spirit to help us to walk as Jesus walked as discussed in this sermon, would the Church of Christ and even the whole world not be turned into a little paradise. Most Christians know the value of these attributes but societal and economic pressures are forcing them to live contrary to these truths. So what must we also do after learning, discussing and seeing these truths in the practical life of Jesus our Master. Let the Holy Spirit be our help and support in this area also! Amen!

9
Text: 1 John 2:6
Theme: Walking as Christ Walked (V)

INTRODUCTION

Virtues describing our right conduct both spiritually and practically are rare to find today. Virtues of purity and holy conduct are downtrodden in the modern society. So are virtues governing and exalting appropriate and sound practical character. Jesus dealt with these in His own practical life and conduct during His earthly ministry and in His teaching ministry to help us. Some of the virtues He encouraged and emphasized in this area to help us can be discussed in this and the next sermon with the following details:

DISCUSSION

I. WE ARE ENJOINED TO FOLLOW HOLINESS AND PURITY

(Matthew 5:8; Philippians 4:8; 1 Timothy 1:5; 5:22; James 4:8)

II. WE ARE ENCOURAGED TO WALK WITH ABSOLUTE PERSUASION

(Philippians 4:13)

III. WE ARE EXHORTED TO WALK WITH A BOLD AND HOPEFUL ATTITUDE

(Psalm 119:28; Matthew 3:17; John 14:1; 1 Thessalonians 5:11-14)

IV. WE ARE TO WALK BY BEING AVAILABLE

(Mark 1:17-18; Acts 16:10)

V. WE ARE TO WALK WITH CLOSE ATTENTIVENESS

(Hebrews 2:1)

CONCLUSION

Sound conduct at the personal level, at the societal level and in business relationships cannot be over-emphasized in the lives of all the genuine children of Christ. This is one way the Holy Spirit can make us stand out as God's people in this crooked and perverse generation within which we are commanded to shine as lights. Let the principles of Christ outlined in this sermon help us to do this in the power of the Holy Spirit.

10
Text: 1 John 2:6
Theme: Walking as Christ walked (VI)

INTRODUCTION
Virtues describing our right conduct both spiritually and practically are rare to find today. Virtues of purity and holy conduct are downtrodden in the modern society. So are virtues governing and exalting appropriate and sound practical character. Jesus dealt with these in His own practical life and conduct during His earthly ministry and in His teaching ministry to help us. Additional virtues He encouraged and emphasized in this area to help us can be discussed in this sermon with the following details:

DISCUSSION
I.   WE ARE TO WALK IN WISDOM WITH DISCERNMENT
     (1 Kings 3:9; Psalm 119:97–98)
II. WE ARE TO WALK IN DILIGENCE
     (Proverbs 10:4; Colossians 3:23)
III. WE ARE TO WALK BY HAVING INITIATIVE AND DYNAMISM
     (Proverbs 22:29; Philippians 3:14; 4:13–15)
IV. WE MUST ALWAYS WALK WITH GREAT EMPATHY
     (Job 29:13; Isaiah 40:11; Mark 1:41; Luke 19:4; 1 Peter 3:8)
V. WE ARE TO WALK IN FULL ENTHUSIASM
     (Matthew 5:16; Romans 12:11; Galatians 6:9; Colossians 3:23)

CONCLUSION

Sound conduct at the personal level, at the societal level and in business relationships cannot be over-emphasized in the lives of all the genuine children of Christ. This is one way the Holy Spirit can make us stand out as God's people in this crooked and perverse generation within which we are commanded to shine as lights. Let the principles of Christ outlined in this sermon help us to do this in the power of the Holy Spirit.

11
Text: 1 John 2:6
Theme: Walking as Christ walked (VII)

INTRODUCTION
The mind matters very much in everything we do as Christians. With it, we are able to examine all facts before applying them. With it, we are able to accept Christ and the salvation He offers. With it, we are able to analyse the Scriptures to be able to apply their truths to our lives. So, the mind is of vital importance in the Christian experience. This is why the use of the mind in the different areas of the Christian Life is emphasized throughout this sermon with some of the following specific details which we are going to discuss in this and the next sermon in this way:

DISCUSSION
I.   WE MUST ALWAYS BE THOUGHTFUL AND DECISIVE
     (Philippians 2:4)
II. WE MUST ALWAYS WALK BY EXERCISING SOUND DISCRETION
     (Psalm 90:12; Ephesians 4:23; 5:15–16; 1 Peter 4:10)
III. WE MUST ALWAYS WALK WITH PROPER DEMEANOUR
     (Psalm 112:5; Proverbs 22:3; Romans 12:2; 14:19)
IV. WE MUST ALWAYS WALK IN GREAT OPTIMISM
     (Luke 21:17-19; John 16:33; Romans 8:25)
V.   WE MUST ALWAYS WALK IN TOTAL OBEDIENCE
     (Deuteronomy 13:4; Proverbs 19:16; John 14:15; 15:14; 2 Corinthians 10:5)

CONCLUSION

We want to conclude this sermon by re-emphasizing the last point which says we must always walk with the mind to obey and being good examples. This sums up all the truths discussed above. The mind truly matters. So if we walk with the sound mind required in all situations and apply all the principles discussed in this sermon, we shall surely please the Lord and further become successful in whatever we do.

12
Text: 1 John 2:6
Theme: Walking as Christ walked (VIII)

INTRODUCTION
The mind matters very much in everything we do as Christians. With it, we are able to examine all facts before applying them. With it, we are able to accept Christ and the salvation He offers. With it, we are able to analyse the Scriptures to be able to apply their truths to our lives. So, the mind is of vital importance in the Christian experience. This is why the use of the mind in the different areas of the Christian Life is re-emphasized throughout this sermon with some of the following additional specific details:

DISCUSSION
I. WE MUST ALWAYS WALK BY BEING PERFECTLY AGREEABLE
   (Amos 3:3)
II. WE MUST ALWAYS WALK WITH GREAT APPRECIATION
   (Romans 12:10)
III. WE MUST ALWAYS WALK WITH A GOOD ATTITUDE
   (James 1:19)
IV. WE MUST ALWAYS WALK WITH THE MIND OF BEING GOOD AND ALTRUISTIC
   (1 Peter 2:21,22; 2:12, 15, 17)
V. WE MUST ALWAYS WALK WITH THE MIND OF BEING ACCEPTABLE
   (1 Peter 2:13–14)

CONCLUSION

The mind truly matters. So, if we walk with the sound mind required in all situations and apply all the principles discussed in this sermon, we shall surely please the Lord and further become successful in whatever we will do. May we once again appeal to the Blessed Holy Spirit to help us in this direction.

13

Text: 1 John 2:6

Theme: Walking as Christ walked (IX)

INTRODUCTION

Character development like the normal growth of a human being is always progressive because of man's imperfection since the Fall. But when we determine to walk with God, the Holy Spirit helps us to develop the appropriate character that goes with this high and holy calling of Christ. Several character traits are going to be discussed in this and the next sermon which are traits which give credence to the truth that we are moving steadily towards the appropriate practical and spiritual nature which God desires. Let us look at these positive character traits in this first sermon as follows:

DISCUSSION

I. WE MUST WALK WITH THE FAITH OF A CHILD
    (Matthew 18:2-4) (Luke 18:16, 17)

II. WE MUST WALK WITH PERFECT COMMITMENT
    (1 Timothy 6:20) (2 Thessalonians 2:15)

III. WE MUST WALK TO BE COMMUNICATIVE
    (1 Timothy 4:12) (Titus 2:7, 8)

IV. WE MUST WALK WITH CONSTANT CONVICTION
    (Daniel 1:8) (Acts 11:23)

V. WE MUST WALK TO DEMONSTRATE CHRISTIAN COOPERATIVENESS
    (Ephesians 4:3) (2 Corinthians 13:11)

CONCLUSION

Whenever we talk about Christian maturity, it also involves perfect character development and sound practical conduct. When the New Life in Christ begins spiritually in us after the New Birth, it develops to a point of acceptable practical Christian maturity. If we want to know whether we are maturing and moving towards God's character ideals, the character traits prescribed by Christ and discussed in these two sermons can be the acid test. How are you personally faring in this? Is it acceptable to you to be acceptable to outsiders and those around you? May the Holy Spirit continue to be our helper!

14
Text: 1 John 2:6
Theme: Walking as Christ walked (X)

INTRODUCTION

Character development like the normal growth of a human being is always progressive because of man's imperfection since the Fall. But when we determine to walk with God, the Holy Spirit helps us to develop the appropriate character that goes with this high and holy calling of Christ. Several character traits such as were discussed in the previous sermon are further going to be discussed in this second sermon to help us ascertain and be sure that we are moving steadily towards the appropriate practical and spiritual nature which God desires. Let us look at some of these additional positive character traits as follows:

DISCUSSION

I.   WE MUST WALK AS PEOPLE WHO ARE CREATIVE AND DEVICEFUL
     (1 Timothy 4:14) (2 Timothy 1:6)
II. WE MUST WALK WITH DILIGENCE
     (Colossians 3:23) (Ephesians 6:6-7)
III. WE MUST WALK AS PEOPLE WHO ARE DEPENDABLE
     (Colossians 1:10) (Philippians 1:27)
IV. We must walk with Determination
     (Psalms 119:30; 2 Timothy 4:7,8)
V.   WE MUST ALWAYS WALK WITH PERFECT DEFERENCE
     (Romans 14:21; 15:1,2)

CONCLUSION

Whenever we talk about Christian maturity, it also involves perfect character development and sound practical conduct. When the New Life in Christ begins spiritually in us after the New Birth, it develops to a point of acceptable practical Christian maturity. If we want to know whether we are maturing and moving towards God's character ideals, the character traits prescribed by Christ and discussed in these two sermons can be the acid test. How are you personally faring in this? Is it acceptable to you to be acceptable to outsiders and those around you? May the Holy Spirit continue to be our helper!

15

Text: 1 Peter 2:21

Theme: Walking in the Steps of Christ (I)

INTRODUCTION

Whenever character develops and reaches an acceptable maturity level, it brings us to a point where we begin to walk in the steps of Christ. Walking in the steps of Christ involves the maturity of character which remains resilient in the face of temptations and seductions into sin and evil. Such a character is also able to develop strong defence against the tempter called Satan and all his wiles. Such a character has some of the following important characteristics which we are going to discuss in this and the next sermon. It includes the following facts:

DISCUSSION

I. WE START LIVING AS PEOPLE WHO ARE TRULY DEVOTED

(Colossians 3:2) (Philippians 3:19, 20)

II. WE START LIVING AS PEOPLE WHO HAVE PERFECT DISCERNMENT

(1 Samuel 16:7; Proverbs 19:2)

III. WE START LIVING AS PEOPLE WHO ARE DISCREET

(Ephesians 4:29) (Colossians 4:6)

IV. WE START LIVING AS PEOPLE WHO ARE VERY DISCIPLINED

(1 Timothy 4:7) (Titus 2:12)

V. WE START LIVING AS PEOPLE WHO ARE ALWAYS DECISIVE

(Colossians 3:10) (Ephesians 4:22, 24)

CONCLUSION

Are these character traits which provide the evidence for true maturity and spiritual growth seen in your life as a Christian as you go through this sermon? When a child always remains a child, then there is something wrong with its physical development. When a Christian always remains a spiritual babe in Christ without growing spiritually to be able to exhibit the character traits of maturity such as are discussed in this sermon, then truly, there is something wrong with his spiritual growth and development which also needs to be probed and corrected. The truths discussed in this sermon can provide the practical basis for such a spiritual probing.

16
Text: 1 Peter 2:21
Theme: Walking in the Steps of Christ (II)

INTRODUCTION

Whenever character develops and reaches an acceptable maturity level, it brings us to a point where we begin to walk in the steps of Christ. Walking in the steps of Christ involves the maturity of character which remains resilient in the face of temptations and seductions into sin and evil. Such a character is also able to develop strong defence against the tempter called Satan and all his wiles. Such a character has some of the following important additional characteristics which we are going to discuss together with those in the previous sermon. It includes the following additional facts:

DISCUSSION:

I. WE START LIVING AS PEOPLE WHO ARE FREE FROM SINS OF THE MOUTH LIKE SWEARING AND SLANDERING (James 1:26) (Ephesians 4:29)

II. WE START LIVING AS PEOPLE WHO HAVE STRONG ENDURANCE IN SACRIFICE (Galatians 6:9) (2 Thessalonians 3:13)

III. WE START LIVING AS PEOPLE WHO TRULY HAVE GODLY PRIORITIES IN SALVATION (Matthew 6:33; 19:29)

IV. WE START LIVING AS PEOPLE WHO ARE FEARLESS (2 Timothy 1:7) (Romans 8:15)

V. WE START LIVING AS PEOPLE WHO ARE FLEXIBLE (Philippians 4:12, 13) (2 Corinthians 6:4-6)

CONCLUSION

Are these character traits which provide the evidence for true maturity and spiritual growth seen in your life as a Christian as you go through this sermon? When a child always remains a child, then there is something wrong with its physical development. When a Christian always remains a spiritual babe in Christ without growing spiritually to be able to exhibit the character traits of maturity such as are discussed in these two sermons, then truly, there is something wrong with his spiritual growth and development which also needs to be probed and corrected. The truths discussed in these two sermons can provide the practical basis for such a spiritual probing.

17

Text: 1 Peter 2:21

Theme: Walking in the Steps of Christ (III)

INTRODUCTION

Another major sign of spiritual maturity is the ability to walk in truthfulness and integrity with the help of the Holy Spirit. This is what will make the church both the salt and the light of the world. Truthfulness is really missing in the world today. But it is the responsibility of the church and its mature and faithful members to help re-establish this truth in our chaotic world. This sermon and the next one which will follow it deal with some of the traits of this truthfulness and integrity as Christ taught and demonstrated them during His earthly ministry. These include interesting facts like the following:

DISCUSSION

I.   WE HAVE TO WALK IN GOD'S GRACE
     (Psalm 94:11; James 4:6)
II. WE HAVE TO FOLLOW GODLINESS
     (3 John 1:11) (Philippians 3:17)
III. WE HAVE TO SEEK AND FOLLOW GOD'S GUIDANCE
     (John 16:13) (Exodus 13:21)
IV. WE HAVE TO SEEK AND FOLLOW HARMLESSNESS
     (Heb. 7:26) (Philippians 2:14, 15)
V.   WE HAVE TO WALK IN HONOUR
     (Philippians 2:3) (Romans 12:10)

CONCLUSION

Walking in Godliness, truthfulness and integrity is possible. But this is possible only within the limits of God's grace. This is the reason why we need to cultivate these attitudes by always seeking and totally depending upon God's grace. When this is done constantly, we can even go beyond our targets and projections with the help of the Holy Spirit.

18
Text: 1 Peter 2:21
Theme: Walking in the Steps of Christ (IV)

INTRODUCTION
Another major sign of spiritual maturity is the ability to walk in truthfulness and integrity with the help of the Holy Spirit. This is what will make the church both the salt and the light of the world. Truthfulness is really missing in the world today. But it is the responsibility of the church and its mature and faithful members to help re-establish this truth in our chaotic world. This sermon like the previous one is going to deal with additional traits of this truthfulness and integrity as Christ taught and demonstrated them during His earthly ministry. These include interesting facts like the following:

DISCUSSION
I.   WE HAVE TO FOLLOW PRUDENT HOSPITALITY
     (Romans 12:13) (1 Peter 4:9)
II. WE HAVE TO WALK WITH PERFECT HONESTY
     (Psalm 78:72) (2 Timothy 2:15)
III. WE HAVE TO BE JUST AND HONOURABLE
     (Genesis 6:9) (Hebrews 11:7)
IV. WE HAVE TO WALK WITH MUTUAL SUPPORT AND LOYALTY
     (1 Thessalonians 5:11) (Ephesians 4:12)
V.   WE HAVE TO WALK WITH MEEKNESS AND LOWLINESS
     (Psalms 62:5) (2 Corinthians 3:5)

CONCLUSION

Walking in Godliness, truthfulness and integrity is possible. But this is possible only within the limits of God's grace. This is the reason why we need to cultivate these attitudes by always seeking and totally depending upon God's grace. When this is done constantly, we can even go beyond our targets and projections with the help of the Holy Spirit.

19

Text: 1 Peter 2:21

Theme: Walking in the Steps of Christ (V)

INTRODUCTION

Another important sign of spiritual maturity is the state in which we are able to maintain the heart in times of emotional stress, in times of pressure, in times of persecution and trials and generally, in times of hardships and sufferings. The heart is the seat of all our affections, the centre of all our emotions and the source of all our actions. So, if our spiritual maturity does not affect it, then it has gone only skin-deep without any deep roots. It is the good state of the heart which can bring us constant survival. To help us to know how best to handle the heart in the process of maturity, we want to discuss some essential facts on this truth in this sermon and the next one which will follow it with the following details:

DISCUSSION

I. WE MUST GROW TO BE PITIFUL
    (Luke 6:36) (Ephesians 5:1, 2)

II. WE MUST GROW TO BE PATIENT
    (Romans 12:12) (Colossians 1:11)

III. WE MUST GROW IN CONSTANT PERSEVERANCE
    (Galatians 6:9) (1 Corinthians 15:58)

IV. BEFORE OPPONENTS, WE MUST BE STRONG AND PERSUASIVE
    (2 Timothy 2:25) (1 Peter 3:15)

V. IN ALL SITUATIONS, WE MUST LEARN TO BE PROMPT
    (Ecclesiastes 3:1) (Ephesians 5:15, 16)

CONCLUSION

The heart is important to our existence and survival in the world. This is why Proverbs 4:23 gives us this piece of advice on its best condition: *"Keep your heart with all diligence, for out of it spring the issues of life."* NKJV; *"Guard your heart above all else, for it determines the course of your life."* NLT. Let the truths discussed in this sermon help us to guard our hearts above every other thing to ensure our success and constant progress.

20

Text: 1 Peter 2:21

Theme: Walking in the Steps of Christ (VI)

INTRODUCTION

Another important sign of spiritual maturity is the state in which we are able to maintain the heart in times of emotional stress, in times of pressure, in times of persecution and trials and generally, in times of hardships and sufferings. The heart is the seat of all our affections, the centre of all our emotions and the source of all our actions. So, if our spiritual maturity does not affect it, then it has gone only skin-deep without any deep roots. It is the good state of the heart which can bring us constant survival. To help us to know how best to handle the heart in the process of maturity, we want to discuss some more essential facts on this truth in this sermon with the following details:

DISCUSSION

I. WE MUST ALWAYS LEARN TO EXERCISE PRUDENCE (Proverbs 13:6; Proverbs 22:3)

II. WE MUST ALWAYS AIM AT FULFILLING OUR PURPOSE (Philippians 3:13, 14) (Hebrews 12:1)

III. WE MUST ALWAYS WALK TO BE RESPECTFUL AND PERSEVERING
(1 Thessalonians 5:12-14) (Revelation 2:3)

IV. WE MUST ALWAYS WALK WITH A FAIR SENSE OF SECURITY AND PROTECTION (Proverbs 29:25; John 6:27)

V. WE MUST WALK IN TOTAL SUBMISSIVENESS AND PLAINNESS (Ephesians 5:21) (Galatians 5:13)

CONCLUSION

The heart is important to our existence and survival in the world. This is why Proverbs 4:23 gives us this piece of advice on its best condition: *"Keep your heart with all diligence, for out of it spring the issues of life."* NKJV; *"Guard your heart above all else, for it determines the course of your life."* NLT. Let the additional truths discussed in this second sermon also help us to guard our hearts above every other thing to ensure our success and constant progress.

21

Text: 1 Peter 2:21

Theme: Walking in the Steps of Christ (VII)

INTRODUCTION

In God's kingdom, there is only one Lord who is the Triune God. All others, be them spiritual beings or ordinary human beings are servants. Knowing the essential qualities of servanthood is therefore of utmost importance to us all. This and the next sermon following it put together some of these important qualities of servant-leaders which are required to make them successful. They incorporate the following essentials taught by Jesus as follows:

DISCUSSION

I. WE MUST BEGIN WITH SELF-ACCEPTANCE
(2 Corinthians 12:9–10) (Ephesians 3:16)

II. WE MUST UNDERSTAND AND WORK WITH SELFLESSNESS
(Titus 2:14) (Ephesians 2:10)

III. WE MUST UNDERSTAND AND WORK WITH TOTAL SENSITIVITY
(Romans 12:15) (1 Corinthians 12:26)

IV. WE MUST UNDERSTAND OUR ROLE AS SERVANT-LEADERS
(Luke 22:26) (1 Peter 5:3, 4)

V. WE MUST DETERMINE TO WORK WITH ALL SINCERITY
(Joshua 24:14; 1 Peter 1:22)

CONCLUSION

Servant leaders are servant workers in God's Holy Kingdom whose work is very important to the building of the Kingdom of God. As such, their work is distinct with several requirements of practical selfless qualities and sacrificial motives. In summary, it is walking in the steps of Christ in leadership. We therefore need to exhibit all the essential qualities of servanthood discussed in this sermon to be successful.

22
Text: 1 Peter 2:21
Theme: Walking in the Steps of Christ (VIII)

INTRODUCTION

In God's kingdom, there is only one Lord who is the Triune God. All others, be them spiritual beings or ordinary human beings are servants. Knowing the essential qualities of servanthood is therefore of utmost importance to us all. In this second sermon, as we did in the previous one, we are going to put together some more of these important qualities of servant-leaders which are required to make them successful. They incorporate the following essentials taught by Jesus as follows:

DISCUSSION
I. WE MUST DETERMINE TO WORK TO BE SUCCESSFUL
    (Matthew 25:21) (Luke 16:10)
II. WE MUST UNDERSTAND THAT SOMETIMES THE WORK INVOLVES SUFFERING
    (1 Peter 4:1) (Galatians 5:24)
III. WE MUST UNDERSTAND THAT OUR WORK IS MAINLY SUPPORTIVE
    (Galatians 6:2) (1 Corinthians 9:22)
IV. WE MUST KNOW THAT THE WORK REQUIRES TACTFULNESS
    (Colossians 4:6) (Ephesians 4:29)
V. WE MUST KNOW THAT THE WORK ALSO INVOLVES TEACHING
    (Matthew 7:28; 28:19–20; John 7:16; Mark 4:2; 2 John 1:9)

CONCLUSION

Servant leaders are servant workers in God's Holy Kingdom whose work is very important to the building of the Kingdom of God. As such, their work is distinct with several requirements of practical selfless qualities and sacrificial motives. In summary, it is walking in the steps of Christ in leadership. We therefore need to exhibit all the essential qualities of servanthood discussed in this sermon.

23
Text: 1 Peter 2:21
Theme: Walking in the Steps of Christ (IX)

INTRODUCTION

This sermon groups more of the qualities required of servant leaders to make them successful in what God has called them to do. Even though the Holy Spirit is our main helper and supporter in ministry, we also need these practical qualities to help us to perform since the work is going to be done among human beings who need to see certain genuine human qualities before they can openly accept us as genuine messengers of Christ. The additional qualities as taught and exemplified by Christ in His public ministry can be grouped together in this sermon as follows:

DISCUSSION
I.   WE NEED TO BE TEMPERATE
     (Titus 2:12) (Romans 6:12)
II. WE NEED TO BE TOLERANT
     (Ephesians 4:2) (Romans 14:1)
III. TO BE EFFICIENT, WE NEED THOROUGHNESS
     (Ecclesiastes 9:10; Colossians 3:23)
IV. WE ALWAYS NEED TO WORK WITH TIME
     (Psalm 90:12) (Ephesians 5:16, 17)

CONCLUSION

The work of the Lord Jesus in God's kingdom of righteousness is unique and therefore it requires special qualities and special levels of commitment. The reason is that, work in God's kingdom is the only ministry which has both present and future implications affecting our present lives on earth as human beings, and at the same time preparing us for future spiritual lives in God's Holy Kingdom after our death. We therefore need to be apt to this task in all areas. May the facts of this sermon help us.

24

Text: 1 Peter 2:21

Theme: Walking in the Steps of Christ (X)

INTRODUCTION

This sermon groups more of the qualities required of servant leaders to make them successful in what God has called them to do. Even though the Holy Spirit is our main helper and supporter in ministry, we also need these practical qualities to help us to perform since the work is going to be done among human beings who need to see certain genuine human qualities before they can openly accept us as genuine messengers of Christ. The additional qualities as taught and exemplified by Christ in His public ministry can be grouped together in this sermon as follows:

DISCUSSION

I.   WE ALWAYS NEED TO WORK WITH UNDERSTANDING AND KNOW-HOW
     (Psalms 119:34) (James 1:5)

II. WE ALWAYS NEED TO WORK TO PROMOTE SPIRITUAL KNOWLEDGE
     (Colossians 3:12–17) (Ephesians 4:31, 32)

III. WE ALWAYS NEED TO WORK AS SERVANTS WITH ZEAL AND KEENNESS
     (Luke 2:49; John 2:17; John 8:29)

IV. WE NEED TO BE SERVANTS WHO ARE KNOWLEDGEABLE
     (2 Timothy 2:15) (Hosea 4:6a)

CONCLUSION

The work of the Lord Jesus in God's kingdom of righteousness is unique and therefore it requires special qualities and special levels of commitment. The reason is that, work in God's kingdom is the only ministry which has both present and future implications affecting our present lives on earth as human beings, and at the same time preparing us for future spiritual lives in God's Holy Kingdom after our death. We therefore need to be apt to this task in all areas. May the facts of this sermon help us.

25

Text: Mark 10:45

Theme: Some Essential Leadership requirements for the true Servants of Christ (I)

INTRODUCTION

Apart from dying to save us from the power of sin when He came into the world as the Son of Man, the Lord Jesus Christ through His own leadership style and teaching ministry provided a pattern for sound and faithful leadership in the Church He came to establish by His sacrificial death on the cross. Jesus knew after His death and resurrection, His church made up of saved people was going to be built by His faithful servants called the Apostles which would require spiritual and practical leadership at all levels. So some of the teachings Christ offered in the Gospels were meant to equip and support these future leaders to be able to take up the leadership roles in the church.

This sermon and the next one which will follow it have put together some of these special teachings reserved for leaders to make them efficient in their work for Christ. Though the facts presented in these sermons are not exhaustive, they include the following essential ones which all genuine spiritual leaders need.

DISCUSSION

I.   All Spiritual leaders need to be Compassionate
     (Matthew 9:36) (Hebrews 4:15; 5:1, 2)
II. All true spiritual leaders must fully be Committed
     (Luke 9:62) (Hebrews 10:38)
III. All true spiritual leaders must see themselves as Servants

(Mark 10:45) (Matthew 20:28)

IV. All true Spiritual leaders must always be Loving and Sympathetic
(Colossians 3:14; 1 Corinthians 13:13)

V. All true Spiritual leaders must always be Forgiving and Spiritually Supportive
(Luke 23:34) (1 Peter 3:9)

CONCLUSION

The world and the church of Christ need role models in leadership. But the best role model we can have who lived to demonstrate all these virtues discussed above is the Lord Jesus Christ. So we need more of Jesus in the world of leadership than any other role model. When we imitate Christ, we will not only be able to live out these virtues discussed above but we will always become successful in our leadership task. Let us therefore imitate Christ as leaders!

26

Text: Mark 10:45

Theme: Some Essential Leadership requirements for the true Servants of Christ (II)

INTRODUCTION

Apart from dying to save us from the power of sin when He came into the world as the Son of Man, the Lord Jesus Christ through His own leadership style and teaching ministry provided a pattern for sound and faithful leadership in the Church He came to establish by His sacrificial death on the cross. Jesus knew after His death and resurrection, His church made up of saved people was going to be built by His faithful servants called the Apostles which would require spiritual and practical leadership at all levels. So some of the teachings Christ offered in the Gospels were meant to equip and support these future leaders to be able to take up the leadership roles in the church.

This sermon like the previous one has put together some additional special teachings reserved for leaders to make them efficient in their work for Christ. Though the facts presented in these sermons are not exhaustive, they include the following essential ones which all genuine spiritual leaders need.

DISCUSSION
I. ALL TRUE SPIRITUAL LEADERS MUST BE VERY PRAYERFUL
    (Psalm 32:6) (Luke 6:12)
II. ALL TRUE SPIRITUAL LEADERS MUST ALWAYS EXHIBIT EXTREME PATIENCE

(Galatians 6:9; Colossians 3:12))

III. ALL TRUE SPIRITUAL LEADERS MUST BE GENTLE AND SUPPLIANT

(Philippians 4:5) (Titus 3:2)

IV. ALL TRUE SPIRITUAL LEADERS MUST ALWAYS EXERCISE SELF-CONTROL

(Titus 1:8; 2:6-8)

V. ALL TRUE SPIRITUAL LEADERS MUST ALWAYS BE HUMBLE AND SOBERMINDED

(1 Thessalonians 5:6) (1 Peter 5:8; James 4:10)

CONCLUSION

The world and the church of Christ need role models in leadership. But the best role model we can have who lived to demonstrate all these virtues discussed above is the Lord Jesus Christ. So we need more of Jesus in the world of leadership than any other role model. When we imitate Christ, we will not only be able to live out these virtues discussed above but we will always become successful in our leadership task. Let us therefore imitate Christ as leaders!

27
Text: Matthew 14:23
Theme: Jesus' Lessons on Prayer

INTRODUCTION
Metaphorically, prayer has been described as the breath of believers. Just as without breathing even for a short moment we shall all die, so shall we all die spiritually if we do not pray regularly for strength, power and direction. The Lord Jesus Christ emphasized these truths for us throughout His earthly ministry. In fact, we can say that He began His ministry with prayer and ended it with prayer. By this He left us the best example and challenge on prayer. If Jesus prayed constantly when He came into our sinful world, then who are we to neglect prayer and think of success. We can learn the following lessons from the Lord Jesus Christ on prayer in this sermon.

DISCUSSION
I. JESUS PRAYED THROUGHOUT HIS EARTHLY MINISTRY
    1) He always prayed in secret for power. (Matthew 14:23; Mark 1:35; 6:46; Luke 5:16; 6:12; 9:18, 28, 29)
    2) He often prayed to perform the works of God. (John 11:41, 42)
II. JESUS PRAYED FOR HIS FUTURE MINISTERS
    1) He prayed for Apostle Peter. (Luke 22:32)
    2) He prayed for believers in general. (John 17:20-26)

III. JESUS PRAYED UNTIL THE END OF HIS MINISTRY

1) He prayed in Gethsemane to be able to face the cross. (Matthew 26:36-39; Mark 14:32-35; Luke 22:41-44; Hebrews 5:7)
2) He prayed before He died on the cross. (Matthew 27:46; Luke 23:34, 46)

CONCLUSION

Whatever Jesus did on earth during His earthly ministry, He did it to leave us an example of what we can also do and should do. We give ourselves to service because Jesus served as our example throughout His earthly ministry. We pray for healing and miracles because Jesus did the same thing in His ministry. We preach repentance and salvation because Jesus did the same thing throughout His earthly ministry. We teach in the church today because Jesus moved everywhere as a great teacher. If we do all these things today because Jesus did them, why should we neglect prayer which Jesus gave himself to throughout His earthly ministry? Do we have any tangible excuses not to pray constantly today? Not at all. We must learn to pray at dawn, to pray in the morning, to pray in the afternoon, to pray in the evening and to pray at night because prayer is our vital breath.

> Psalm 55:16-17
> *"But I will call on God, and the LORD will save me.*
> *Morning, noon, and night I cry out in my distress, and*
> *the LORD hears my voice"* NLT

28

Text: Matthew 28:18

Theme: Manifestation of God's Power in the Life and Ministry of Jesus

INTRODUCTION

One great lesson we must all learn from Jesus whether we are His workers or ordinary Christians in His church is the importance of seeking, receiving and maintaining God's power in our lives. We should remember that we are only flesh and blood created from the dust of the earth. As a result, our sufficiency always comes from God and from His mighty power. This is the reason why we must always seek and rely absolutely on God's power in everything we will do exactly as Jesus did. Jesus has shown us the way by teaching and showing us what can happen when God's power remains upon us all the time. Some of the truths can be discussed in this sermon as follows:

DISCUSSION

I. THE POWER OF THE LORD JESUS WAS MANIFESTED IN THE WORLD
    1) It was manifested as absolute power. (Matthew 28:18; John 10:17, 18, 28; 17:2; Philippians 3:20, 21; 2 Thessalonians 1:9; 1 Timothy 6:16; 2 Peter 1:16; Revelation 3:7; 5:12)
    2) It was manifested in the salvation of men. (Hebrews 7:25)
    3) It was manifested in His forgiving sins. (Matthew 9:2, 6; Mark 2:5, 10; Luke 5:20, 24; Colossians 3:13)

II. THE POWER OF THE LORD JESUS WAS MANIFESTED IN HIS WORKS

1) It was manifested in creation. (John 1:3, 10; Colossians 1:16)

2) It was manifested in the casting out of demons. (Matthew 8:16; 12:28, 29; Mark 3:27; Luke 11:20-22)

3) It was manifested in His healing of diseases. (Matthew 8:3, 16; 9:6, 7; 12:13; Mark 5:27-34; Luke 5:17; 6:19; Acts 10:38)

III. THE POWER OF THE LORD JESUS WAS MANIFESTED IN HIS WORKERS

1) It was manifested in His imparting healing power to the apostles. (Matthew 10:1; Mark 6:7; Luke 9:11)

IV. THE POWER OF THE LORD JESUS WAS MANIFESTED IN HIS WONDERS

1) It manifests in His upholding all things. (Colossians 1:17; Hebrews 1:3)

2) It manifested in His stilling the tempest. (Matthew 8:27)

3) It manifested in His resurrection. (John 2:19; 10:17, 18)

CONCLUSION

If God's power is so essential to our existence and in our ministries, then why are so many people not seeking this power today but are rather resorting to demonic sources of power? First, it is because the Bible has predicted that demonism and demon worship will characterize this end-time period. Secondly, it is because God's power is not cheap but always demands purity and holiness of life before it is imparted. So which way are you turning as far as the power of God is concerned? Will you start seeking it earnestly today by fulfilling the conditions attached to it or you are also going to go the way of the world as most people are doing in this end-time period?

29

Text: Isaiah 41:13

Theme: Relying on the Promises of Christ

INTRODUCTION

The help we receive from Christ did not end with His earthly ministry because He has promised to be with us always until the end of the age. This is what the text chosen from Isaiah 41:13 echoes in the words, *"Fear not, I will help you."* What are some of the specific things Christ promised to do to help us during and after His earthly ministry? Though the list will be too long to exhaust in a short sermon like this, at least we can mention the following:

DISCUSSION

I.   CHRIST HAS PROMISED US THE HELP OF THE HOLY SPIRIT

1) He has promised us the Holy Spirit as our comforter. (John 14:16, 26; 15:26, 27; 16:7-14)

2) He has promised us the power of the Holy Spirit. (Luke 24:49; John 7:38, 39; Acts 1:4-8)

II. CHRIST HAS PROMISED US HIS OWN HELP AS GOD'S SON

1) He has promised us his help as our mediator. (John 16:23, 24, 26, 27)

2) He has promised us His everlasting life. (Matthew 19:28; Mark 10:29, 30; Luke 18:29, 30; 23:43; John 5:25-29; 6:54, 57, 58; 12:25, 26)

CONCLUSION

Are there any promises from Christ which can be greater than the few discussed in this sermon? When you have the Holy Spirit and the Lord Jesus Christ Himself with you, then you have the whole Godhead in your life and activities. What else can be greater than these? May we see the fulfilment of these promises constantly in our lives as Christians and Christian workers. Amen!

30

Text: John 8:46

Theme: Learning from the Holiness of the Lord Jesus Christ

INTRODUCTION

One important character of the Lord Jesus Christ which offers a great challenge to all His true and faithful followers is His absolute holiness and sinlessness while on earth. His friends and close confidants saw and admitted this during His earthly ministry. His die-hard enemies also saw and admitted this as well as even demons who always called Him the holy One of God. This character of Christ offers His children one of the greatest challenges in Practical Christianity which is made possible only by the enablement of the Holy Spirit through the New Birth. What character lessons can we learn from this holy nature of Christ today? Let the facts in this sermon help us as follows:

DISCUSSION

I.   THE HOLINESS OF THE LORD JESUS WAS FORETOLD (Psalm 45:7; Isaiah 11:4, 5; Jeremiah 23:5; Zechariah 9:9)

II. THE HOLINESS OF THE LORD JESUS WAS FULFILLED (John 5:30; 7:18; 8:46; 14:30; Revelation 3:7)

III. THE HOLINESS OF THE LORD JESUS WAS DEMONSTRATED BY HIS FAITHFULNESS (Isaiah 11:5; Luke 4:43; John 7:18; 8:29; 9:4; 14:3; 17:8; Hebrews 3:2; Revelation 1:5; 3:14, Hebrews 2:17)

CONCLUSION

Christianity is sometimes rejected by some people not because it does not make sense. But just because its moral demands are high. Matthew 5:48 will tell you to strive towards the perfection of God Himself as soon as you become a Christian in the words, *"Be perfect, therefore, as your heavenly Father is perfect."* NIV; *But you are to be perfect, even as your Father in heaven is perfect"* NLT. Because of passages like this and many others, some people shy away from Christianity. But the Holy Spirit is the one who helps us to attain this ideal of holiness. So let us turn to Him for Him to help us to move towards this holiness and perfection of Christ discussed in this sermon.

31
Text: 2 Corinthians 5:13, 14
Theme: Knowing the Content and Scope of the Love of Christ

INTRODUCTION
Love is another virtue which is lost in the world today. The extreme secularization in the world today is fast replacing love with hatred in the lifes of many people. Hatred leading to wickedness and sometimes even to bloodshed is eulogized by many people. What has gone wrong spiritually to cause this? Another important lesson which we can learn from Christ in this sermon is love and how it must be demonstrated in practical terms to make it useful and beneficial to the world. What does Christ have to teach us on this? It is as follows:

DISCUSSION
I. CHRIST SHOWED DEEP LOVE FOR HIS DISCIPLES AND CONFIDANTS
    (John 10:3, 4, 11, 14-16; 13:1, 23; 14:21; 15:9-13, 15; Romans 8:35, 37-39; 2 Thessalonians 2:13)
II. CHRIST SHOWED DEEP LOVE FOR CHILDREN
    (Matthew 19:13-15; Mark 10:13, 14, 16; Luke 18:15, 16)
III. CHRIST SHOWED DEEP LOVE IN HIS CRUCIFIXION
    (2 Corinthians 8:9; Philippians 2:6-8) (Galatians 2:20; Ephesians 5:2, 25, 29, 30; 1 John 3:16; Revelation 1:5)
IV. CHRIST SHOWED DEEP LOVE FOR THE LOST AND CONFUSED
    (Isaiah 40:11; Matthew 18:12, 13; Luke 13:34) (Isaiah 53:4; Matthew 8:17; Romans 15:3) (Psalm 72:14; Isaiah 63:9)

CONCLUSION

The world is crying for love! Families are crying for love! Children are crying for love! Those who are spiritually lost are crying for love. But where can this love be found? It can only be found in the Lord Jesus Christ. He is calling on all to come to Him for a taste of this supreme love. Will you turn to Him today? It is neither too late nor shameful to do this because we need this love which only Christ can show and impart to us.

32

Text: Matthew 9:36
Theme: The Compassion of the Lord Jesus Christ

INTRODUCTION
Compassion is the attitude of having pity for people and showing them concern to alleviate their suffering to bring them peace and comfort. This is an attitude which the suffering world needs now. It is also needed in the church of the Lord Jesus Christ. But unfortunately, it is an attitude which is fast disappearing from the world and even from the Church of Christ. The modern society is becoming more and more egocentric and people care for themselves and their needs without showing any concern to others. Perhaps this is because things are getting harder and harder in the world. But we need to learn precious lessons from Christ on this as Christians and be different from the world. What precious lessons does the life of Christ offer us on compassion? At least we can learn the following from the character of Christ on compassion.

DISCUSSION
I. CHRIST SHOWED COMPASSION FOR THOSE WHO WERE SPIRITUALLY DISTRESSED
(Isaiah 42:3; Matthew 9:36; 12:20; 18:12, 13; 23:37; Luke 13:34; Mark 1:41; 6:34; Luke 7:13; 15:4-9, 20-24; 19:41, 42; John 11:33-38; 18:8, 9; 2 Corinthians 8:9; Hebrews 4:15; 5:2)

II. CHRIST SHOWED COMPASSION FOR THOSE WHO WERE PHYSICALLY DESTITUTE

(Isaiah 53:4; Matthew 8:3, 16, 17; 14:14; 15:32; 20:34; Mark 8:2, 3)

III. CHRIST SHOWED COMPASSION THROUGH HIS DEFERENCE

(Luke 22:27; John 13:5, 14; 2 Corinthians 8:9; Philippians 2:7, 8; Hebrews 2:11)

CONCLUSION

We must all admit that in our generation we can say that we are in a suffering world which suffering has come about as a result of the increase in sin, lawlessness, and a mass falling away which have been predicted to characterize the end-time period in which we find ourselves today. But this does not prevent us from showing and bringing Christ's compassion to people. Let us pray to be able to walk in the steps of Christ to possess and show the compassion He had as we have learnt in this sermon.

33

Text: Isaiah 53:7

Theme: Learning from the Meekness of Christ

INTRODUCTION

A meek person is that person who maintains a quiet, gentle and calm disposition, not willing to fight or argue noisily in the face of provocations. Meekness is not foolishness. Foolishness is the inability to show good judgement in situations which demand the display of a high sense of wisdom. Very often, some people mistakenly equate foolishness with meekness but the two are not the same. A meek person is a sensible Christian who is wise in all the things of God but who for the sake of Christ and the gospel is not willing to get involved in any altercation with lost sinners and unregenerated people in the light of scriptural passages like 2 Timothy 2:24. *"And the Lord's servant must not be quarrelsome but must be kind to everyone, able to teach, not resentful."* NIV.

There were many things Christ in His omnipotence could have done to His enemies and false accusers but would that have helped fulfil God's redemptive plan for mankind? That was why He had to adopt this attitude of meekness to help fulfil God's great plan for lost humanity. Christ Jesus is the source and repository of wisdom. He knew what He was doing by being meek and silent before His enemies and false accusers. As Christians we have a lot of lessons to learn from the meekness of the Lord Jesus from this sermon. Let us look at the details as follows:

DISCUSSION

I. THE MEEKNESS OF CHRIST WAS PREDICTED
(Psalm 45:4; Isaiah 42:1-3; 50:5, 6; 52:1, 14; 53:7; Matthew 12:19, 20; 21:5; Acts 8:32)

II. THE MEEKNESS OF CHRIST WAS PORTRAYED
1) It was portrayed in not resenting false accusation. (Mark 2:6-11)
2) It was portrayed in submitting to enemies. (Matthew 26:47-63; 27:12-14; John 8:48-50; Hebrews 12:2, 3; 1 Peter 2:23)
3) It was portrayed in praying for enemies. (Luke 23:34)
4) It was portrayed in becoming a servant. (Philippians 2:7)

CONCLUSION

As Christians walking in the steps of Christ, how and where can we also demonstrate the meekness of Christ in practical terms to further the gospel? This can take place in many ways including our relationship with our pastors, our attitude in lay leadership, in our marital affairs and in our attitude towards our fellow believers in the church. If Christ has shown us the way, let us walk in His steps with the help of the Holy Spirit. Amen.

34

Text: Philippians 2:9-11

Theme: Knowing the Special Power and Authority in the Name of Jesus

INTRODUCTION

Spiritually, physically and practically, the name of the Lord Jesus Christ is the greatest and most powerful name everywhere – in heaven, on earth, under the earth and under the sea! The evidence is seen whenever and wherever genuine servants of God who are filled by the genuine Holy Spirit mention this name authoritatively wherever Satan and his demons are operating. They flee instantly in different directions because of the superlative and compelling power in this name.

In fact, by raising the name of Jesus to this level of power and authority, our great and living God has left the Church of the Lord Jesus Christ a great legacy which must be protected with holy living and faithful profession of faith. While it cannot be possible to talk about everything the name of Jesus does and can do in a single sermon like this one, at least mentioning some of the important benefits that we can derive from the power of this great name such as we are going to discuss in this sermon is worthwhile. It includes the following details:

DISCUSSION

I. THE NAME OF THE LORD JESUS HAS SUPERNATURAL POWER
    1. The name of the Lord Jesus has Superlative Power. (Phil. 2:9; Matt. 28 :18)

2. The name of the Lord Jesus has Living Power. (Mark 5:40-42; Acts 9:40; 20:9-10)
3. The name of the Lord Jesus has Subjugating Power. (Phil. 2:10-11; Ps. 108:13; Ps. 44:4)
4. The name of the Lord Jesus has prevailing Power. (John 14:13-14; John 15:7; 16:24)
5. The Name of the Lord Jesus has Special Power. (Acts 5:15; 19:11-12)

II. THE NAME OF THE LORD JESUS FULFILLS SPECIAL PURPOSES
1. The name of the Lord Jesus has Saving Power. (Acts 4:12; Jn. 14:6 Luke 24:47)
2. The name of the Lord Jesus has Transforming Power. (Acts 9:4-5, 21-25)
3. The name of the Lord Jesus has Deliverance Power. (Luke 10:1-12 with Luke 10:17-20; Luke 9:49-50; Mk. 9:38-41)
4. The name of the Lord Jesus has Healing Power. (Acts 3:5; Acts 3:16)

CONCLUSION

After going through this sermon and considering the great power and authority in the name of Jesus, is there anything that this great power and authority in the name of Jesus exercised by genuine servants and messengers cannot do? The answer is a big no. It is able to make a way where there is no way, bring dead persons back to life, perform supernatural miracles where necessary, bring us victory in times of difficulties and above all save our souls. Let us conclude by asking ourselves this question: Have you considered this name for your salvation and all the other great benefits it brings?

JOHN

1

Text: Matthew 4:21, 22

Theme: Apostle John's call and commitment

INTRODUCTION

Like all other disciples who later became apostles, John was also specially called by Christ to fulfil a great ministry which he did not initially know. In his walk with Christ, he became fully committed to Him which made God use him fully as He has planned for his life. The details of his call and commitment can be discussed in this sermon as follows:

DISCUSSION

I.   JOHN RECEIVED A SPECIAL DIVINE CALL
     1. He was called by Christ. (Mark 1:19, 20; Matthew 4:22)
II. JOHN EXHIBITED GREAT ZEAL AND CONFIDENCE
     1. John showed great zeal and confidence in the way he left all immediately and followed Jesus. (Matthew 4:21, 22)
III. JOHN BECAME ONE OF JESUS' CLOSE CONFIDANTS
     1. John intimately associated with Jesus. (John 13:23-26; 21:20)

CONCLUSION

God is and has always been a God of purpose. This means He always has a reason and a specific purpose for doing whatever

He does. But He never reveals all His plans and purposes at once. They are always revealed progressively as we have discussed about Apostle John in this sermon. Have you ever sat down to ponder over why God called you into His great Church? Do this because He always has a plan and purpose for whatever He does. So we can say with all confidence that He called you for a purpose like Apostle John. Which purpose must be fulfilled in your life before He calls you home one day.

2
Text: John 13:23-26
Theme: Meeting John the Apostle

INTRODUCTION
Apostle John was one Apostle who started with Jesus like many of the ordinary disciples but gradually became transformed into a loving and sympathetic worker of Christ. He was one person who loved to be close to Jesus all the time – an attitude which brought him great spiritual advantages. Let us look at a brief analysis of his life and character in this sermon.

DISCUSSION
I.   JOHN STARTED WITH CHRIST AS A HOT-HEADED MAN
   1. This means that, initially, he was a man who was either easily excited or angered. (Mark 3:17)
II. JOHN AGAIN, STARTED WITH CHRIST AS AN AMBITIOUS MAN (Mark 10:28; 9:34)
III. TOGETHER WITH THE ELEVEN, JOHN BECAME AN ACTIVE MISSIONARY (Acts 2:14-15)
IV. FOR HIS DEVOTION TO CHRIST, JOHN BECAME KNOWN AS THE BELOVED DISCIPLE (John 13:23)
V.   FOR HIS DEVOTION TO CHRIST, JOHN BECAME A SPECIAL DISCIPLE (John 13:23)

CONCLUSION
Though Apostle John began with Christ as a hot-headed man. After some time, he became a caring and faithful disciple. Apostle John's relationship with Jesus changed his nature and character completely from a hot-headed man to a cool-headed

Apostle. So drastic and dramatic was this change in John that later, he became the patient and beloved disciple who could care for God's flock. Has your walk with Jesus produced any change in your former life like John? If no, it is not too late. Let us continue to walk in this consciousness and 2 Corinthians 5:17 will become real in our lives.

<u>2 Corinthians 5:17</u>
Therefore, if anyone is in Christ, he is a new creation; old things have passed away; behold, all things have become new. NKJV

3

Text: Matthew 4:21

Theme: The family background of Apostle John

Introduction

In this sermon, we want to look briefly at the family background of Apostle John. Very often, who a person is in life is greatly determined by where he comes from as well as the family which nurtured him into adulthood. Apostle John was one person who had an illustrious family background to make it possible for him to be nurtured by Christ after his call to be one of His greatest disciples and Apostles. Let us look briefly at his family background and history in this sermon which we are going to discuss with the following facts and details:

DISCUSSION

I. APOSTLE JOHN HAD A GOOD FAMILY HISTORY
    1. John probably grew up in Bethsaida which was a fishing town at the northern tip of the Sea of Galilee (John 1:44). This was also the hometown of Philip, Andrew and Peter (John 1:44)
    2. John's family was probably respected and well known in the Judean society and as such he was personally acquainted with the high priest. (John 18:15)
    3. John had at least one brother whose name was James. (Matthew 4:21)
    4. James was also one of the twelve disciples and a member of the inner three. (Matthew 17:1)
    5. About 44 AD James was executed by Herod Agrippa I. (Acts 12:1-2)

II. APOSTLE JOHN HAD A GOOD PARENTAL HISTORY
   1. John, his brother and his father were all fishermen. His
       father's name was Zebedee. (Matthew 4:21, Mark 1:19;
       John 21:2)
   2. It looks like John's father was a wealthy man. He was
       wealthy enough to hire servants to help mend his nets.
       (Mark 1:19-20)
   3. His mother's name was Salome who was the sister of
       Mary, the mother of Jesus. This makes John a first cousin
       to Jesus. (Matthew 27:56; Mark 15:40; 16:1; John 19:25)
   4. Salome was well off and was one of those who
       contributed to the support of Jesus. (cf. Mark 15:40-41;
       Luke 8:3)
   5. Another indication of her wealth is that she could buy
       expensive spices for Jesus' burial. (Mark 16:1)

CONCLUSION

Whether a tree can grow to be a good tree or a bad tree depends
upon the type of seed that is planted in the soil. If you plant a
good orange or mango seed, very soon, you will start harvesting
very sweet fruits. But if instead of these good seeds you plant
thorns and thistles in the same soil, it will not be long before you
start harvesting these thorns and thistles. The seed we are talking
about here symbolically stands for the family seed. Apostle John
came from a good family seed and therefore he could be trained
and used by Christ to fulfil an important future ministry. How is
life in our own families also?

4

Text: Mark 1:19

Theme: The major episodes in the Life and History of Apostle
John

INTRODUCTION

Apostle John's name means "The Grace of Jehovah". John was the beloved disciple of Jesus whose life history offers us some of the best examples of commitment and tenacity right from the day Christ called him to be a disciple up to the day he was called home by the same Lord. Apostle John clung to his master with devotion and singleness of purpose. He truly lived up to his name by seeing God's grace in his call and ministry. Some of the important facts of his life and ministry which we would want to look at in this sermon include the following:

DISCUSSION

I. APOSTLE JOHN HAD A POWERFUL MINISTRY FOR CHRIST

1) John was about five years younger than Jesus (Jensen, 461). He started working in the ministry when he was about 25 years old and died in the ministry at the age of about 100 years (Jensen, 177).

2) He was called by Jesus like all the other disciples. (Matthew 4:21)

3) John wrote the Gospel of John. Ten years later, he was cast into a cauldron of boiling oil for preaching the gospel. By a miracle he remained unharmed.

4) Following this, the Roman emperor Domitian sentenced John to exile. While exiled on the Isle of Patmos he wrote the Book of Revelation. (Jensen, 177).

II. APOSTLE JOHN HAD A POWERFUL MINISTRY IN THE CHURCH

1) John returned from exile and exercised oversight over the churches in Asia (Eusebius 105, Robertson, 1). John strengthened all the existing churches, appointed some to ministry as directed by the Holy Spirit and even started some churches in Asia Minor during this time.

2) He lived into the reign of the emperor Trajan (Eusebius, 105). John died and was buried in Ephesus (Eusebius, 116).

CONCLUSION

Apostle John's life offers us lessons both as Christians and workers as his life history has shown us in this sermon. In fact, Christ did not train him for nothing. He trained and hardened him for a purpose which was partly to make him stand as an example to many and also prepare him to be able to write His important books which form part of the New Testament Canon namely the Gospel of John, the book of Revelation and the books of first, second and third John. How can we also stand today and do what Apostle John did to glorify Jesus? (Mk 1:20; Jn 1:35)

5

Text: John 21:20, 23-24 with Luke 9:54

Theme: Some Positive Character Traits of Apostle John

INTRODUCTION

If Christ could use John mightily in the ministry, part of this depended upon the nature and character of Apostle John. There were several important character qualities which made this possible including those we are going to discuss in this sermon as follows:

DISCUSSION

I. JOHN WAS A FAITHFUL SERVANT

1. John is known as the "Apostle of Love." He really loved the church and always encouraged the brethren to love each other. (1 John 4:7-11)

2. He also succeeded by always being very close to Jesus. (John 13:23)

3. He was one of the first disciples to follow Jesus, he overhead John the Baptist talking about Jesus and he went after him. (John 1:35, 40)

II. JOHN WAS A BOLD AND COURAGEOUS SERVANT

1. Apostle John was brave enough to stand at the foot of the cross; when all the other apostles had fled and were still in hiding. (John 19:25, 26)

2. John could also be trusted; Jesus gave him charge of his mother. (John 19:26, 27)

3. Apostle John gathered courage and was at the present at the trial of Jesus. (John 18:15, 16)

CONCLUSION

Without doubt, Apostle John had a very good nature and character which made Christ use him as He did. Some of these positive character traits discussed in this sermon are worth emulating. But this must be done together with our avoiding some of the negative character tendencies which are also discussed in this sermon.

6

Text: John 21:20,23-24

Theme: Some Practical Character Qualities of Apostle John

INTRODUCTION

John the Great Apostle had some excellent character qualities which could be described as useful practical traits in the ministry of the Lord Jesus Christ today. These traits came together to make John who he was as a valuable tool in the hands of his great master Jesus. Some of these practical traits can be discussed in this sermon as follows:

DISCUSSION

I. JOHN WORKED AS A FAITHFUL SERVANT
    1. John was humble. In his writings he called himself the "disciple whom Jesus Loved." (John 21:20; 23-24)
    2. John together with Peter was bold and confident in replying to the Jewish Council, when they said something like "Whether it is right for us to obey God or man you be the judge, we will obey God." (Acts 4:19)
    3. John worked as a "servant" to Jesus. Jesus could trust him and send him together with Peter to go and prepare the Passover meal for their group and they did. (Luke 22:8)

II. APOSTLE JOHN WORKED AS A WELL-TRAINED SERVICE MAN
    1. Apostle John was present at the healing of Apostle Peter's Mother-In-Law. (Mark 1:29-31)
    2. Apostle John was present at the raising of the daughter of Jairus. (Mark 5:37; Luke 8:51)

3. Apostle John witnessed the two draughts of fishes. (Luke 5:10; John 21:1-7)
4. Apostle John was present at the Transfiguration of Christ. (Matthew 17:1; Mark 9:2: Luke 9:28)

CONCLUSION

Some Bible expositors called Apostle John, "John the Practical Apostle." By this description, they always mean Apostle John was concerned with the actual doings and performance of something rather than theorising about something. Truly, that was a good nature whose proof we have seen and have discussed in this sermon. Can you also be described as a practical man or woman like John. It is one important character trait we all need as faithful followers of Christ.

7

Text: Revelation 1:9, 10

Theme: Some Spiritual Character Qualities of Apostle John

INTRODUCTION

Two major spiritual character qualities which are always very essential for our success as workers and servants of Christ are prayer and a thorough knowledge of the Word of God. The Holy Spirit can never fully use us if we are spiritually deficient in these two major spiritual areas. Spiritually, Apostle John excelled in these two areas to enable the Holy Spirit use him fully to the glory of God. Prove of this can be seen in his life and ministry as we are going to discuss in this sermon as follows:

DISCUSSION

I. APOSTLE JOHN WAS A MIGHTY MAN OF PRAYER AND SOLICITING

1) John was a man of prayer. Jesus took him up the Mount of Transfiguration (i.e. Mount Tabor) to pray. (Luke 9:28)

2) Also, on the Mount of Olives Jesus asked John to pray with Him. (Mark 14:33)

3) John also went to the temple to pray. (Acts 3:1)

4) He received the visions and revelations in the Book of Revelation through prayer. (Revelation 1:1, 2)

II. APOSTLE JOHN WAS A MAN WHO WAS MIGHTY IN THE SCRIPTURES

1) John was a man who studied and knew the scriptures very well. Throughout his gospel he proves how Jesus fulfilled the scriptures. For instance, he quotes: "Zeal for Your house has eaten Me up." (John 2:17)

2) He knew the scriptures in a deep and personal way. (John 2:22)

3) In fact, John was so in tune with the scriptures that he was able to call Jesus "the Word and the Word was God" (John 1:1)

4) He wrote to the Churches based upon the sound truths of God. (John 21:25)

CONCLUSION

When we look at Apostle John's spiritual performance in these two spiritual areas, what does he deserve? Does he deserve commendation or condemnation. Certainly, he deserves commendation. What practical examples can we learn from him then? The Holy Spirit is waiting to use all of us to the glory of God in the great church of our Lord and Saviour Jesus Christ. But we need to prepare the ground for this through prayer and regular intake of God's Word. Let Apostle John show us the way again.

8

Text: Mark 9:38

Theme: Some Negative Character Traits of Apostle John

INTRODUCTION

Apart from the Lord Jesus Christ, there is no other person who can be described as absolutely perfect without any flaws in his life, behaviour and conduct. Apostle John had a lot of positive character traits and qualities but he also had his negative side in the few situations we are going to discuss in this sermon as follows:

DISCUSSION

I. APOSTLE JOHN HAD A FIERY PERSONALITY
1) We don't have many things to say about John having many negative character traits.
2) But one thing we can say for sure is that John did have an explosive or fiery personality.
3) It was for this reason that Jesus gave him and his brother the name, "Sons of Thunder." (Mark 3:17; Luke 9:52-56)
4) One time John and his brother wanted to call fire down from heaven upon somebody for using Jesus' name in ministry. But Jesus rebuked them for this attitude (Mark 9:38-40)

II. APOSTLE   JOHN   HAD   AN   OVER-AMBITIOUS PERSONALITY
1) John was also overzealous to protect Jesus' ministry and interest. But Jesus told him that it was alright if someone, not in their team, was casting out demons in His name (Mark 9:38, Luke 9:49, 50)

2) Again, John and his brother also offended the other
   apostles because they and their mother asked Jesus if they
   could sit at His left and right-hand side in glory. (Mark
   10:35-41)
3) Apostle John can be said to be intolerant by some of these
   negative character traits exhibited above (Mark 9:38)
   (Luke 9:51-55)

CONCLUSION

Jesus always loves us and is forever willing to use us in ministry
to glorify His name when we exhibit genuine penitence and
submission when He rebukes us to correct us. He is all-knowing
and knows all His servants through and through so His
corrections are always true and justified. If we submit to His
corrections and rebukes all the time, no negative character traits
can hold Him back from using us to glorify His name as He has
planned. The life of Apostle John bears clear testimony to this.

9

Text: Acts 4:1, 2 with Galatians 2:9

Theme: Apostle John's Companions and his Positive Contributions

INTRODUCTION

Apostle John was exposed to some people and other people were also exposed to him in his normal and ministry life. Naturally, this brought him some experiences which made such a positive impact upon his life that he was encouraged to persevere with Christ up to the end. These encounters further produced a commitment in him which drove him to labour for God in His church. Let us look at the details on this in this sermon.

DISCUSSION

I. APOSTLE JOHN HAD HIS CHIEF COMPANIONS

1. One major encounter he had was with God Himself at the Transfiguration (Matt. 17:1; Mark 9:2; Luke 9:28)

2. Another great encounter he had was with Christ at the foot of the cross. (John 19:26-27)

3. Another great encounter John had was when Jesus appeared to him on the Isle of Patmos. (Revelation 1:9)

4. Another great personality around John was his brother, James, who was a prominent personality in the early church. (Galatians 2:9; Luke 9:54)

5. John also spent a lot of time with another close companion, Apostle Peter. They went on missions together, prayed together, worked miracles together and even stood before the Sanhedrin together. (Acts 4:1; 8:14-15)

6. Apart from John and James sometimes getting into trouble together, these companions were for the most part great influences on each other. (Mark 10:35-41; Luke 9:54)

7. Initially, he also spent some time with John the Baptist, who exerted a major godly influence upon his life. John the Apostle was a follower of John the Baptist before the Savior began His ministry. (John 1:15)

II. APOSTLE JOHN MADE SOME GOOD CONTRIBUTIONS TO GOD'S CAUSE

1. Apostle John had a powerful and positive ministry influence upon the early church in Jerusalem and at Ephesus. (Acts 3:1, 3)

2. Apostle John also had a great influence in Samaria and upon the Christians in the surrounding areas of Jerusalem, Galilee and Ephesus. (Acts 8:14, 15)

3. Through his writings, he has made a great impact upon the church right from its early development in Jerusalem up to the present day. (John 21:25)

4. John endorsed Apostle Paul by his acknowledging God's grace was upon him in the ministry of the Church. (Galatians 2:9)

CONCLUSION

Who are your companions in Christ. What influence are they exerting on you? Is it positive or negative? What lessons can you learn from Apostle John on this from this sermon. God always wants us to associate with people who can exert a positive influence upon our lives to help us to become more committed to Him and to His course like Apostle John. So be careful with those you associate with both in life and in ministry!

10

Text: Mark 1:29-31

Theme: Lessons from the Powerful school of John

INTRODUCTION

One of the things Jesus took John through during the period of his training as a disciple was the witness of His great power. He called John to be present at most of the manifestations of His great power to prepare Him for His future ministry which required great faith and a reliance upon this great power for success. Let us look at the exhibitions of Jesus' great power in the presence of John in this sermon as follows:

DISCUSSION

I.   JOHN WAS A WITNESS OF JESUS' HEALING POWER

1. He saw the healing of Peter's mother-in-law. (Mark 1:29-31)

II. JOHN WAS A WITNESS OF JESUS' MIRACLE WORKING POWER

1. He was a witness of the raising of Jairus' daughter. (Mark 5:37; Luke 8:51)

2. He saw the miracle of the two draughts of fishes. (John 21:1-7; Luke 5:9-10)

III. JOHN WAS A WITNESS OF JESUS' DIVINE POWER

1. He was present at the transfiguration of Jesus. (Matthew 17:1; Mark 9:2; Luke 9:28)

IV. JOHN WAS A WITNESS OF JESUS' RESURRECTION POWER

1. He saw the empty tomb after the resurrection of Christ. (John 20:2-8)

2. He saw the resurrected Christ at the sea of Galilee. (John
   21:7)

CONCLUSION

The witness of the manifestation of Christ's power as discussed
in this sermon was surely to prepare John for His future and final
ministry. As a young man among the apostles, he lived longer
than all of them. Tradition says that after one of the wicked
Roman emperors had tried unsuccessfully to fry him alive in the
cauldron full of oil, he banished him to the island of Patmos
where he received and recorded what is known today as the book
of Revelation which is the last book of the Bible. Do not be
discouraged by whatever you are going through in the church of
the Lord Jesus Christ and in the ministry of God today. It could
be a special preparation for some great things God wants to do
with you.

JOHN THE BAPTIST

1
Text: Matthew 14:4,8
Theme: Powerful lessons from John the Baptist to us today

INTRODUCTION
One great challenge in the ministry is knowing your call, sticking to it and finishing with it. Many potentially good workers in the church are sometimes confused about this creating major problems for themselves and for the church of the Lord Jesus Christ but John the Baptist was not like that. When he learnt from his parents the purpose and circumstances of his birth, he decided to live to fulfil God's plan. Let us learn the facts on this from this sermon.

DISCUSSION
I.   JOHN'S MINISTRY DAYS WERE DESTINED BY THE LORD
     (Luke 1:41)
II. JOHN THE BAPTIST GREW UP AND ANSWERED THE
     CALL OF THE LORD
     (Luke 1:76-77, 80)
III. JOHN THEREAFTER SET HIS HEART FIRMLY ON THE
     LORD (Luke 1:80a; 3:2)
IV. JOHN THE BAPTIST BECAME A STRONG BUT HUMBLE
     LEADER
     (Matthew 3:11; Luke 3:3)

V. JOHN LIVED HIS ENTIRE LIFE TO POINT OTHERS TO
THE LORD
(John 3:30)
VI. JOHN THE BAPTIST LOVED THE TRUTH AND
DEFENDED IT WITH HIS LIFE
(Matthew 14:8)

CONCLUSION

As we can learn from the facts above, John's life first
demonstrates the importance of knowing what you want to do in
the ministry. Secondly, it demonstrates the importance of doing
what you want to do according to the principles of God. Thirdly,
it demonstrates the importance of remaining firmly committed to
your call even if it means death. We have a lot to learn from John
as called ministers of the Lord Jesus today.

2

Text: Romans 1:16; 1 Corinthians 9:22

Theme: Some essential Spiritual Lessons from the life of John the Baptist

INTRODUCTION

The call of John and the circumstances surrounding his birth and ministry are full of precious lessons for us today. These are lessons which touch on our relationship with God, on our attitude in ministry and on our general behaviour and conduct as Christians. Let us glean some of these truths in this sermon as follows:

DISCUSSION

I.   NOTHING IS IMPOSSIBLE WITH GOD
      (Luke 1:5-7, 11-13)
II.   WE SHOULD NEVER DOUBT GOD
      (Luke 1:18-20)
III. BEING IN A CHRISTIAN HOME DOES NOT MEAN YOU SHOULD JOKE WITH GOD
      (Proverbs 22:6; Ephesians 2:8-9)
IV.   SPEAKING THE TRUTH ALWAYS PLEASES GOD
      (Romans 1:16; 1 Corinthians 9:22)
V.   THERE IS JOY IN A LIFE OF TOTAL DEVOTION TO GOD
      (Matthew 3:4)
VI.   THERE IS THE NEED FOR CONSTANT SELF-EXAMINATION IN OUR WALK WITH GOD (Matthew 3:10; 2 Corinthians 13:5)
V.   THERE IS THE NEED TO `MAINTAIN HUMILITY BEFORE GOD

CONCLUSION

God will always be God because He is a God from eternity to eternity. Because of His omnipotence, none of His pre-determined plans and purposes can be thwarted. It had been prophesized that Jesus was going to have a forerunner who was going to prepare the way before Him as the Messiah. So John the Baptist had to come and fulfil this by the omnipotent power of God. Let us not doubt God when He moves to fulfil His words because His pre-determined plans and purposes can never be thwarted.

3

Text: Luke 1:13

Theme: The background of John the Baptist

INTRODUCTION

The two major characteristics of John's life which are full of lessons for us today are his birth and his ministry background. His birth was eventful just as his ministry was. His birth was pre-arranged by God in line with prophecy. His ministry as predicted by God was in connection with Jesus' coming. When the two combine, then we have John the Baptist as God projected him to be. Let us look at some of the details in this sermon.

DISCUSSION

I. JOHN HAD A NOTABLE AND PURPOSEFUL BIRTH
1. His real name is John meaning "God is gracious."
2. His patents were Elizabeth and Zachariah the Priest. (Luke 1:13)
3. Both of John's parents were from the tribe of Levi and descended from Aaron. (Luke 1:5)
4. Therefore John was a Levite and in the priestly line of Aaron. (Luke 1:5c)

II. JOHN HAD A GOOD MINISTRY BACKGROUD
1. John was born as the forerunner to the Lord Jesus. (Matthew 3:3)
2. John had the privilege of baptizing the Lord Jesus. (John 1:29-34; Matthew 3:13-17)
3. Jesus maintained a high level of respect for John. (Luke 7:28)
4. John died a noble death for the truth. (Matthew 14:1-12)

CONCLUSION

John keeps on emphasizing in his ministry to the Jews that being a Hebrew was not an automatic guarantee of personal salvation. So he used strong words like *"You brood of vipers"* and others to drum this home to his people and to rouse them out of their complacency and spiritual lethargy. Today, his life and ministry are giving us the same message. Our being in a church or coming from a Christian family does not guarantee us automatic personal salvation. So if the Jews needed to repent personally before receiving the salvation of God, so do we also need to repent and be converted before we can have access to the salvation offered by Christ through His death.

4

Text: Matthew 3:7

Theme: A Brief summary of Ministry Lessons we can learn from John the Baptist I

INTRODUCTION

As far as the ministry of the Lord Jesus Christ is concerned, there is no end to knowledge. Because the ministry always presents new challenges, there is the need to seek knowledge and fresh insight from the Lord all the time. This is the only way we can excel in the ministry and stand where the Holy Spirit can continue to use us to bring glory to God. The first part of the summary of truths and precious lessons we can learn from John the Baptist in this sermon is meant to help us in this regard. The details are as follows:

DISCUSSION

I.   JOHN WAS CALLED AND CHOSEN FROM BIRTH (Psalm 139:16) (Luke 1:13-15)

II. JOHN MINISTERED AS A MAN WHO WAS FEARLESS AND BOLD

1. John ministered with total boldness and total obedience of heart. (Matthew 3:1-12)

III. JOHN MINISTERED AS A POWERFUL BOND-SERVANT

1. John ministered as a powerful preacher and servant of Christ.

(Mark 1:1-8; John 5:33-35) (Colossians 3:16)

IV. JOHN MINISTERED AS A MAN WHO UNDERSTOOD HUMBLE BROTHERHOOD

1. John ministered as a man Humble in spirit. (John 1:15) (Deuteronomy 18:18) (Matthew 18:4)

CONCLUSION

There are several temptations in the ministry which seek to change our message and direction to be able to please human beings especially the rich, powerful and affluent in the church. But we must never be men pleasers if we want to minister to please the one who called us. This is one great example John the Baptist has left us as ministers and faithful servants of Christ in addition to all the others discussed in this sermon. Can we imitate John and die for the truth just as he did in his ministry?

5

Text: Matthew 3:7

Theme: A Brief summary of Ministry Lessons we can learn from John the Baptist II

INTRODUCTION

As far as the ministry of the Lord Jesus Christ is concerned, there is no end to knowledge. Because the ministry always presents new challenges, there is the need to seek knowledge and fresh insight from the Lord all the time. This is the only way we can excel in the ministry and stand where the Holy Spirit can continue to use us to bring glory to God. This second part of the summary of truths and precious lessons we can learn from John the Baptist in this sermon is meant to help us in this regard. The details are as follows:

DISCUSSION

I. JOHN MINISTERED AS A MAN WHO WAS HOLY IN BEHAVIOUR
   1. John was holy in character. (Matthew 14:1-12; Leviticus 20:7)

II. JOHN MINISTERED AS A MAN WHO WAS CLEAR IN HIS OPEN BROADCAST
   1. John ministered as a man with a clear testimony. (John 3:26-28; 10:40, 41; 1:6-8)

III. YET JOHN MINISTERED AS A MAN WHO WAS NATURAL AND HUMAN IN BATTLE
   (Matthew 4:12; 11:2-6; Luke 7:24-29)

CONCLUSION

There are several temptations in the ministry which seek to change our message and direction to be able to please human beings especially the rich, powerful and affluent in the church. But we must never be men pleasers if we want to minister to please the one who called us. This is one great example John the Baptist has left us as ministers and faithful servants of Christ in addition to all the others discussed in this sermon. Can we imitate John and die for the truth just as he did in his ministry?

JUDAS ISCARIOT

1

Text: 1 Corinthians 10:12

Theme: Judas' call and consecration

INTRODUCTION

There are many controversies about Judas. One of these controversies is the question of his salvation after his call. Some scholars argue that though Judas was a disciple, he was never truly saved. Others argue that Judas was truly called and saved like all the other disciples but he only yielded to the temptations of Satan in connection with the work given to him and fell just as Adam and Eve initially truly belonged to God and even merited His visits to them in the Garden but later yielded to Satan's temptations and fell. Whatever be one's position on this, the long and short of this is that, Judas was called and consecrated like all the other disciples but he could not fulfil his call. Let us look at Judas' call and consecration in this sermon and what lessons we can learn from it.

DISCUSSION

I. JUDAS WAS CALLED LIKE ALL THE OTHER DISCIPLES OF CHRIST
   1. Judas was called into the service of Christ like all His followers. (Matthew 10:2-4; Acts 1:16-17)

2. Judas happily responded to the call like all the other disciples. (Luke 9:57-62)

3. Judas worked and walked with Christ during the first three years of his call. (John 13:29; 12:4-6) (Acts 1:24-26)

II. JUDAS WAS LOVED BY CHRIST LIKE ALL THE OTHER DISCIPLES IN HIS COMPANY

1. Jesus Loved Judas from his call to his very end. (John 6:64, 70-71)

2. Proof of this love was that, he was given a special seat at the Last Supper. (John 13:26)

3. Judas possessed the same grace and miraculous powers like all the other disciples (Matthew 10:1, 8; 12:22)

4. Jesus' prayer for the church and the disciples included Judas. (John 17:6-19)

CONCLUSION

The major lessons of this sermon are that, first, Judas was truly called and consecrated by Christ to holy service like all the other disciples. Secondly, Jesus extended the same love He had for all the disciples to Judas also. If this was the case, why did Judas fall from this high plane of spiritual elevation to this low level of personal and ministry degradation. Maybe the answer lies in the warning, *"Therefore let him who thinks he stands take heed lest he fall."* NKJV (1 Corinthians 10:12)

2

Text: James 1:13-15

Theme: Judas, his fall from Apostleship to Apostasy

INTRODUCTION

There is no Bible character who has become as infamous as Judas. There is a wide gap between apostleship and apostasy. So, Judas falling from apostleship to apostasy through the betrayal of the Lord Jesus to His enemies has brought him this infamy. Exactly how and why Satan could work through Judas remains an enigma among Bible scholars and all sincere Christians because there was nothing to suggest this openly during the first three years of Judas' ministry. But lo and behold, the fall came. Let us look at its details and the lessons we can learn from it in this sermon.

DISCUSSION

I. JUDAS PREPARED THE GROUND FOR HIS OWN FALL
   1. Judas walked as a traitor. (Matthew 26:14-16)
   2. Judas stopped caring like a true disciple. (John 12:6; 1 John 3:17)
   3. Judas walked as a secret thief. (John 12:6)
   4. Judas walked as a complaining disciple. (Matthew 26:8; Mark 14:4) (John 12:4-6)

II. JUDAS TOOK STEPS THAT HASTENED HIS FALL
   1. Judas acted as a backstabber. (Matthew 7:19; John 6:64)
   2. Judas allowed himself to be overcome by temptation. (Matthew 26:25; Luke 22:3-6; John 13:2)
   3. Judas yielded to the sin of betrayal. (Matthew 10:4; Mark 3:19; Luke 6:16; John 6:71)

4. Judas consequently became the son of perdition. (Matthew 27:3; John 17:12; 13:2; Acts 1:25)

CONCLUSION

The Bible emphasizes that whenever we are tempted to sin, we should not think that God is doing this. Rather, we must have the understanding that every temptation begins as a conception of evil in the heart and inner man which after some months comes out as the actual involvement in sin just like a conceived baby is born after nine months. The stages leading to Judas' fall from apostleship to apostasy followed this warning given to us by God. Let us all be wary of lusting after evil in our hearts in secret! It can lead us into outward temptation.

> James 1:13-15
> *"Let no one say when he is tempted, "I am tempted by God"; for God cannot be tempted by evil, nor does He Himself tempt anyone. But each one is tempted when he is drawn away by his own desires and enticed. Then, when desire has conceived, it gives birth to sin; and sin, when it is full-grown, brings forth death."* NKJV

3

Text: 1 Peter 5:8

Theme: Some crucial Spiritual Lessons from the life of Judas

INTRODUCTION

Rather than always condemning Judas for his sin of betrayal, sometimes we should sit down and ask ourselves, what are the spiritual lessons we can learn from the life of Judas to help us avoid his tragic and disgraceful end after being given the full chance to be one of the great Apostles of the Lord Jesus Christ. Temptations similar to what came to Judas and Adam and Eve in the Garden of Eden can come to us also no matter how high we are in the spirit if we walk in negligence and open our door to Satan. What are some of the spiritual lessons we can learn from the life of Judas to help us avoid this completely. Let us look at some of these in this sermon as follows:

DISCUSSION

I. IT IS NEVER POSSIBLE TO SERVE GOD AND MAMMON (John 12:4-6; John 13:29; 1 Timothy 6:10)

II. WHENEVER GOD GIVES US THE CHANCE TO REPENT, WE MUST SEIZE THIS OPPORTUNITY AT THAT MOMENT (Matthew 6:24; Mark 8:36; 1 Timothy 6:10)

III. BEING IN THE CHURCH PHYSICALLY DOES NOT MEAN THAT YOU ARE SPIRITUALLY LISTED AMONG ITS MEMBERSHIP (Matthew 7:21; Luke 6:46; Romans 2:13)

IV. WHENEVER YOU GIVE SATAN YOUR FINGER, HE ALWAYS TAKES OVER YOUR FULL MAN (Luke 22:3; John 13:2; Ephesians 4:26-27)

V. REMORSE AND THE OUTWARD SHEDDING OF TEARS IS
    NOT THE SAME AS MEA-CULPA (Matthew 27:3-5)

CONCLUSION

Whenever we invite Satan into our lives through secret sin, we should never think that he will gloss over this. His main purpose of his moving about like a roaring lion is to seek opportunities to kill, to steal and to destroy those he will get. When Judas created this sinful platform for him to come and stand on to work in his life, he did not miss it! When we also create sinful opportunities for him to attack and destroy us, he will never miss them. So let us always be vigilant and sober as we have learnt in this sermon.

4

Text: 2 Peter 3:17

Theme: Some of the negative characteristics of Judas which led to His fall

INTRODUCTION

There is no person who is absolutely perfect on earth as a human being. All men have their shortcomings and human imperfections. This is what makes it very important for every man to do constant self-examination and introspection to prevent his being stolen spiritually and enslaved by the devil through sin or any other sinful tendencies. This is what Judas failed to do which led to Satan entering his heart and using him to do what was abominable in the sight of God and later destroyed him. Let us look at some of these negative tendencies of Judas in this sermon to serve as a warning to us.

DISCUSSION

I.   JUDAS' SIN AND BETRAYAL WAS FORETOLD (Acts 1:16, 20; John 17:12)

II. JUDAS' SIN AND BETRAYAL WAS FULFILLED (Matthew 26:47-49; John 18:5)

III. JUDAS' SIN AS A BETRAYAL WAS FOMENTED (John 6:70; Mark 14:10-11)

IV. JUDAS' SIN AND BETRAYAL COULD NOT BE CORRECTED WITH MERE REMORSE WITHOUT GENUINE REPENTANCE (Matthew 27:3-5; Acts 1:18)

V. JUDAS' SIN AND BETRAYAL CALLED FOR HIS IMMEDIATE REPLACEMENT (Acts 1:23-26)

CONCLUSION

It is because of our imperfections as human beings no matter how high God has raised us that the Bible constantly admonishes us to beware in passages like 2 Peter 3:17 which reads: *"You therefore, beloved, since you know this beforehand, beware lest you also fall from your own steadfastness, being led away with the error of the wicked."* NKJV. *"You already know these things, dear friends. So be on guard; then you will not be carried away by the errors of these wicked people and lose your own secure footing.* NLT. When Judas failed to pay heed to this warning, what was the result in his life and ministry? If we also fail to pay heed to this warning, what can be the outcome? Let us beware! May the Lord help us in this!

5

Text: 1 Corinthians 15:58

Theme: Summary Outline of the Life of Judas

INTRODUCTION

Like all men on earth, Judas had his early life, his life of service and his terminal life. Every man is judged after his death by what happens in these three important stages of his life. Let us look at the details of Judas' life in these areas.

DISCUSSION

I.   JUDAS HAD HIS EARLY LIFE
     1. Judas' name means "Praise."
     2. Judas was probably born in the Judean city of Kerioth.
     3. Judas began as a called Apostle. (Matthew 10:2-4)
     4. Judas is first mentioned in Matthew 10:4.
II. JUDAS HAD HIS MINISTRY LIFE
     1. Judas initially worked as a potential Apostle. (Matthew 10:2-4; John 13:29)
     2. He is mentioned about 22 times in the New Testament.
     3. He was the apostle who betrayed Christ to the Jews. (Mark 14:10)
III. JUDAS HAD HIS LATTER LIFE
     1. Tradition says that Judas died in and around Jerusalem.
     2. Judas died by hanging himself. (Matthew 27:5; Acts 1:18)
     3. He is finally mentioned in the Scriptures in Acts 1:25.

CONCLUSION

What conclusion should we draw on Judas after looking at these three important stages of his life. Should we call him a success or a failure? What will men write about us after examining our lives in this same way in the future. This is why we should pay heed to 1 Corinthians 15:58 so that we don't become like Judas at the end of our lives. It reads: *"Therefore, my beloved brethren, be steadfast, immovable, always abounding in the work of the Lord, knowing that your labor is not in vain in the Lord."* NKJV. *"So, my dear brothers and sisters, be strong and immovable. Always work enthusiastically for the Lord, for you know that nothing you do for the Lord is ever useless."* NLT

JOSEPH OF ARIMATHEA

1

Text: Luke 23:50-51

Theme: The Background and Spiritual Qualities of Joseph of Arimathea

INTRODUCTION

Though Joseph of Arimathea was one of the secret disciples of Christ, because he lived to fulfil one of the Messianic prophecies relating to the burial of the Lord Jesus Christ, we can say he fulfilled his ministry. His loyalty to Christ can never be questioned because of what he did towards the burial of Christ in defiance of popular opinion. In fact, there is a lot more we can learn from this faithful and secret disciple of Christ in this sermon. The facts are as follows:

DISCUSSION

I. JOSEPH OF ARIMATHEA HAD A GOOD SOCIAL AND SPIRITUAL BACKGROUND

1. He was from Arimathea. (Matthew 27:57; John 19:38a)
2. He was a prominent Jewish leader. (Mark 15:43a)
3. He was wealthy. (Matthew 27:57a; Mark 15:43a) (John 19:41; Matthew 27:60)
4. He cared for Jesus. (John 19:38-40)

II. JOSEPH OF ARIMATHEA HAD A GOOD PRACTICAL
BACKGROUND
1. He was a secret follower of Jesus. (John 19:38, Matthew
27:57)
2. He stood for what was right. (Luke 23:51)
3. He was a good and just man. (Luke 23:50)
4. He was courageous. (Mark 15:43)
5. He was a good planner. (Luke 23:53; Matthew 27:59-61)

CONCLUSION

What is the level of your devotion to the Lord Jesus Christ after coming into the church? Joseph of Arimathea was so devoted to the Lord Jesus Christ that he defied popular societal prejudice to be able to give a befitting burial to the Lord Jesus to remove the shame of His being crucified on the cross like a criminal. He put Jesus in his own new tomb which was very expensive to acquire in those days. If somebody is not totally devoted in heart, can he do this? What can we learn from Joseph here? His life is a big challenge on true devotion to Christ.

2

Text: 1 Corinthians 15:3, 4
Theme: What we can learn from Joseph of Arimathea on what he did for Jesus

INTRODUCTION

It is amazing the way God sometimes uses us as insignificant men made from the dust of the earth to fulfil His great plans and purposes. One man who was used this way was Joseph of Arimathea. Did Joseph know when he was buying this personal tomb that in God's plan it was going to be the burial place of a great person like the Lord Jesus? Yet when God knew that he had a good and willing heart, he used him to fulfil this great purpose which was a prelude to the great resurrection of the Lord Jesus Christ. Let us look at Joseph's credit in this great service.

DISCUSSION

I.   JOSEPH OF ARIMATHEA WAS TOTALLY DEVOTED TO THE LORD JESUS CHRIST
     (Luke 23:51; Romans 6:3)

II. JOSEPH OF ARIMATHEA BROUGHT HONOUR TO THE LORD JESUS CHRIST
     (Matthew 27:58-60; Mark 15:44-46)

II. JOSEPH OF ARIMATHEA PREPARED THE GROUND FOR THE RESURRECTION OF THE LORD JESUS CHRIST
     (1 Corinthians 15:3, 4; Psalm 16:10) (Matthew 28:5-7)

CONCLUSION

It was predestined that Christ had to come into the world to minister, to die, to be buried and to rise from the dead to complete God's plan of salvation for mankind. If it was in God's plan to have Christ buried before His resurrection, then it was in His plan to use somebody to prepare His tomb. When God picked Joseph of Arimathea for this, he fulfilled his part faithfully and brought great honour to His name. What can we also do for God today to help build His kingdom and bring in all those He has planned to save before Christ returns? Let us also do our part with the help of Christ!

JOSEPH, HUSBAND OF MARY

1

Text: Matthew 2:13-15

Theme: Joseph the Good Father

INTRODUCTION

Fathers are plentiful but good fathers are rare to find in many homes. Truly, good fathers always act in the family with concern, love, sacrifice, protective spirit and selflessness. The protection and survival of the family are always their concern. They also provide spiritual and practical leadership in the home to bring glory to God. Such a father was Joseph, the husband of Mary who also became the earthly father of the Lord Jesus. Let us discuss the traits of fatherhood exhibited by Joseph in this sermon as follows:

DISCUSSION

I. JOSEPH LIVED AS AN ORNINARY MAN AS A FATHER
    (Matthew 1:18-19, 20) (1 Corinthians 1:28-29)
II. JOSEPH HAD A PROFESSION AS A FATHER
    (Matthew 13:55; Mark 6:3) (Romans 15:7)
III. JOSEPH USED HIS GIFTS AS A FATHER
    (Matthew 1:24; 2 Peter 1:20-21)

IV. JOSEPH WALKED AS AN OBEDIENT SERVANT AS A FATHER
   (Matthew 1:24-25) (1 Samuel 15:22)
V. JOSEPH WAS PROTECTIVE AS A FATHER
   (Matthew 2:14, 15; Ephesians 6:4)
VI. JOSEPH WAS CONSIDERATE AS A FATHER
   (Luke 2:41-52) (Proverbs 6:20, 23)

CONCLUSION

Looking at the character traits of Joseph discussed in this sermon, shall we not be right to call him a good father? God does not choose vessels for nothing. He always looks out for certain essential qualities first. If God chose Joseph to be the earthly father of the saviour of the whole world, he deserved it. Today, can God get any special spiritual qualities in us to choose and use us as He did in the life of Joseph?

2

Text: Matthew 1:20

Theme: Joseph the Good Husband

INTRODUCTION

Joseph was a good husband by God's standards because he understood God's revelations on marriage at his time but was still prepared to act in obedience to God's special instructions concerning Mary. His action involved social shame and ridicule but he was still prepared to obey God rather than yield to societal pressure.

DISCUSSION

I. JOSEPH WAS A GOOD HUSBAND BY HIS SPIRITUAL BACKGROUND AND BIRTH

1. Joseph was born as a descendent of David and of Abraham. (Matthew 1:1, 2, 16)

2. Joseph took Mary as his wife because he believed the angel in his dream.
    (Matthew 1:18-25)

3. Joseph was not the biological father of Jesus who was born in Bethlehem.
    (Luke 1:34, 35; Matthew 1:25)

II. JOSEPH WAS A GOOD HUSBAND BY HIS PRACTICAL BENEVOLENCE

1. Joseph took his family to Egypt and later back to Nazareth. (Matthew 2:13-15)

2. He took good care of Jesus as a child. (Luke 2:43-46)

3. Joseph became the foster father of Jesus. (Matthew 13:55; Luke 3:23)

CONCLUSION

If you are not a good husband and your wife is impregnated in a mysterious way which has no precedence in history, what will be your natural reaction? What was the reaction of Joseph when Jesus was conceived by the Holy Spirit? This alone qualifies him to be a good husband!

3

Text: Matthew 1:25 with Luke 2:48

Theme: Some Character Strengths and weaknesses of Joseph I

INTRODUCTION

Joseph did what could make God make use of him to be the foster father of Jesus the Messiah but he was an ordinary man born with some of the normal human strengths and weakness. In this sermon we want to discuss some of these strengths and weaknesses as a guide to our own personal conduct today. The details include the following:

DISCUSSION

I. SOME NOTABLE CHARACTER STRENGTHS OF JOSEPH
    1. He was a righteous man. (Matthew 1:19a)
    2. He was Merciful. (Matthew 1:19b)
    3. He was gracious. (Matthew 1:19c)
    4. He was a man who listened to God. (Matthew 1:20, 21, 24, 25)
    5. He was a man who was Obedient. (Matthew 1:25)
    6. He was a man who was Humble. (Matthew 1:20, 24)

II. SOME AVOIDABLE CHARACTER WEAKNESSES OF JOSEPH
    1. He was Presumptuous.
        a) He assumed that Jesus was with His mother and left Him behind. (Luke 2:43, 44)
    2. He was over anxious. (Luke 2:48)

CONCLUSION

As spiritual as he was, Joseph was still a human being. This sermon has shown us that Joseph did not allow his personal weaknesses to outweigh his spiritual qualities. Therefore, he was a man who allowed God to use him to fulfil one of His greatest plans for lost humanity. Do not give up but press on because even God could use abandoned lepers to bring a miracle to Samaria.

4

Text: Matthew 1:25 with Luke 2:48

Theme: Some Character Strengths and weaknesses of Joseph II

INTRODUCTION

Joseph did what could make God use him to be the foster father of Jesus the Messiah. But he was an ordinary man born with some of the normal human strengths and weaknesses. In this sermon we want to discuss some more of these character qualities and strengths as a guide to our own personal conduct today. The details include the following:

DISCUSSION

I. JOSEPH WAS A RESPONSIBLE PARENT
   (Luke 2:51a, 52)

II. JOSEPH AVOIDED PROCRASTINATION
    (Matthew 2:13, 14)

III. JOSEPH UNDERSTOOD FAMILY PROTECTION
     (Luke 2:45; 2:40a)

IV. JOSEPH LIVED AS A MAN WIIO WAS PURE
    (Luke 1:26, 27)

V. JOSEPH WAS SELF-CONTROLLED
   (Matthew 1:25)

VI. JOSEPH WAS A MAN WHO UNDERSTOOD CIVIL COMMANDS
    (Luke 2:1-5)

VII. JOSEPH WAS A MAN WHO WAS CLEVER AND CREATIVE
     (Luke 2:6, 7)

VIII. JOSEPH WAS A MAN WHO WAS OBEDIENT TO
       GOD'S COMMANDMENTS
       (Luke 2:21, 22-24, 39, 41)

CONCLUSION

Though our election by God is by His grace and mercy and when
we are finally chosen by Him to fulfil His purpose, we must do
our best to meet His spiritual and practical standards. This does
not mean that He has chosen us by merit. It is still by His grace
and mercy. But we must act and conduct ourselves in a way
which will not jeopardize what He wants to use us to do. By his
conduct Joseph passed this test to enable God use him to serve
the whole of mankind. What can we also do for God today?

5
Text: Matthew 1:19, 20
Theme: Valuable Life Lessons from Joseph I

INTRODUCTION
Because Joseph was a husband and a parent like all men, some of the things he successfully went through in his marriage and in the society in which he found himself at that time are universal lessons for all men. So we can learn precious life lessons as this sermon seeks to help us to do in the following way:

DISCUSSION
I. HUMILITY IS NEEDED FROM ALL BY GOD (Matthew 1:20, 24)
II. SELF-CONTROL IS NECESSARY TO FULFIL THE PLANS OF GOD (Matthew 1:25)
III. GOD'S DELAYS ARE ALWAYS GOOD (Matthew 1:19, 20)
IV. AS PARENTS, WE SHOULD TEACH OUR CHILDREN TO START WITH GOD
(Luke 2:40, 52)

CONCLUSION
What did Joseph do in this sermon which we are also not required to do as men today. Let us copy all his good examples here in the power of the Holy Spirit to enable God use us in greater ways than He used Joseph to fulfil His great plans and purposes for mankind. Remember that without men like us and Joseph, God will never act to use a man like Judas. So He is still waiting for us.

6

Text: Matthew 1:19, 20

Theme: Valuable Life Lessons from Joseph II

INTRODUCTION

Because Joseph was a husband and a parent like all men, some of the things he successfully went through in his marriage and in the society in which he found himself at that time are universal lessons for all men. So we can learn additional precious life lessons as this second sermon seeks to help us to do in the following way:

DISCUSSION

I. GOD CARES FOR US EVEN IN EMERGENCY SITUATIONS (Matthew 2:13-16)

II. OBEYING GOD IS ALWAYS BETTER THAN SACRIFICE (Matthew 1:19, 20, 24, 25)

III. WE SHOULD BE CAREFUL TO EXERCISE ALL OUR RESPONSIBILITES AS GOD'S TRUE SERVANTS (Luke 2:44-46)

IV. IT IS ALWAYS GOOD TO HANDLE CHILDREN WITH RESTRAINT AND SELF-CONTROL (Luke 2:48-51a)

V. WORK IS A SANCTIFIED SERVICE IN THE SOCIETY (Luke 3:23) (Matthew 13:55a)

CONCLUSION

Life lessons are examples and warnings we get from other people through their actions, inactions, and real-life episodes they go through. Their lives thus become examples to us to guide us and to provide us with the necessary caution in our practical conduct.

Joseph's life lessons which offer both spiritual and practical life lessons can therefore be of immense value to us today as we have learnt from this sermon.

LAZARUS

1
Text: John 11:38-44
Theme: The miracle Lazarus received

INTRODUCTION
It is often said, "God moves in mysterious ways, his wonders to perform!" Because God is highly exalted above us, we can never understand his ways and actions though we can always be sure that all of them will work together for our good. Nobody knows and understands why Lazarus, a good friend of Jesus had to fall sick at this time but thanks be to God that though this sickness was inexplicable, it brought glory to God, shame to the enemies and hope to Lazarus and his sisters. Lazarus' name means "without help". Truly, Lazarus was without help but Jesus became his helper!

DISCUSSION
I.   LAZARUS FELL SICK IN A MYSTERIOUS WAY
     (John 11:1-3)
II. LAZARUS DID NOT IMMEDIATELY GET THE HELP HE WANTED
     (James 1:17) (John 11:5-7; Hebrews 4:15-16)
III. CHRIST DECLARED THE REASON WHY
     (Proverbs 3:5) (John 11:4)
IV. AN UNEXPECTED MIRACLE WAS WAITING

(John 11:38-44) (Matthew 19:26; John 12:1, 9) (Matthew 8:17)
III. ENEMIES DID NOT UNDERSTAND WHY
    (John 11:45-52) (John 11:53; 12:10)
IV. SWEET FELLOWSHIP FOLLOWED THIS WAREFARE
    (John 12:1-2, 17-18) (1 Corinthians 1:9)

CONCLUSION

Lazarus' miracle teaches us that whenever we go into any difficult situation as Christians, it does not mean that God has deserted and abandoned us. As it happened to Lazarus, it could be a way to see His glory and blessings thereafter. As Christ turned the sorrow of Lazarus' sisters to joy, so does He bring us hope in such situations.

2

Text: John 11:44
Theme: Lazarus, the instrument of God's Miracle

INTRODUCTION
Misery can come to us through some of the normal, unfortunate and inexplicable things in life. But whenever this happens, we should never forget Jesus' reassuring statement in Matthew 28:20, ""teaching them to observe all things that I have commanded you; and lo, I am with you always, even to the end of the age." Amen." NKJV. This truth was exemplified in the life of Mary and Martha through the death of their brother Lazarus. The incident goes like this in John's gospel:

DISCUSSION
I.   LAZARUS WAS THE BROTHER OF MARTHA AND MARY
     (John 11:1-4, 5, 6)
II. LAZARUS DIED MYSTERIOUSLY
     (John 11:12-14)
III. BUT JESUS SAVED HIS SISTERS FROM MISERY
     (John 11:41-44)

CONCLUSION
When Jesus promises us of His permanent presence, what are some of the practical implications of this great assurance? What does he want us to derive from this treatment? First, it is to assure us that we are not alone in our struggles and battles. Secondly, it is to assure us of the provisions of His power in all confrontations from Satan and the forces of evil. Finally, it is to assure us of His unfailing victory no matter what happens. When Mary and

Martha trusted Jesus, they saw the benefits of this great presence and glorified God in the end.

LUKE THE PHYSICIAN

1

Text: Colossians 4:14

Theme: Meeting Luke, the Physician

INTRODUCTION

There are times God provides invaluable helpers to support and help His servants in the ministry. Though spiritually He is their support, several physical needs make such helpers necessary. God provided several of such helpers to support Apostle Paul in his ministry including Luke the Physician. Dr Luke was one person who accompanied Apostle Paul on most of his journeys until he finally ended up in Rome. Let us look at some of the notable facts about Luke, the physician.

DISCUSSION

I.   LUKE IS MENTIONED THREE TIMES IN THE BIBLE IN SOME OF THE EPISTLES OF PAUL (Colossians 4:2; 2 Timothy 4:11; Philemon 1:23-24)

II. LUKE WAS A TRAINED PHYSICIAN (Colossians 4:14; Mark 5:26)

III. LUKE WAS VERY HUMBLE IN HIS NATURE AND PURSUITS (Acts 1:1)

IV. LUKE WAS A LOYAL COMPANION OF PAUL

1.   He alone remained with Apostle Paul up to the time of his death. (2 Timothy 4:11)

CONCLUSION

We see in Doctor Luke a mixture and blend of scholarship with important character virtues like humility, gentleness and loyalty. This is something which is very rare in the life of many people today who are always puffed up because of what they know. Dr. Luke sacrificed his profession and remained loyal to the Lord Jesus Christ through the assistance he offered to Apostle Paul in his ministry.

2

Text: Acts 20:5-6
Theme: Some Positive Character Qualities of Luke

INTRODUCTION
Luke did not live as an adult at the time Jesus was born, ministered and died. He emerged as one the second-generation Christians after the resurrection of Christ. His name means "Light-giving". Probably because of the influence of his name, his life offers us several positive character qualities which are a big challenge to us today in the church of Christ today. In fact, the church needs more "Lukes" today to enhance its ministry and outreach. Some of these character traits can be seen as follow

DISCUSSION
I.   LUKE LIVED AS A QUALIFIED CLINICIAN (Colossians 4:14)
II. LUKE LIVED AS A HISTORICAL COMPILER (Luke 1:3, 4; Acts 1:1, 2)
III. LUKE LIVED AS A FAITHFUL COMPANION (2 Timothy 4:11)
V.   LUKE LIVED AS AN ENTHUSIASTIC CRUSADER (Acts 16:10)
VI. LUKE LIVED AS A LOYAL CO-WORKER (Acts 20:5-6)
VII.   LUKE LIVED AS A FAITHFUL COLLEAGUE (Acts 21:1-6)

CONCLUSION
Is there any surprise that the Holy Spirit used Dr. Luke as one of the authors of the New Testament books? He produced two of

the most important books of the New Testament namely, the Gospel of Luke and the Acts of the Apostles. Looking at his life, nature and conduct, if the Holy Spirit used him in this special way, it is normal and fitting.

3

Text: Luke 24:47

Theme: Some of Luke's Character Ideals as seen in His Gospel

INTRODUCTION

Luke's gospel is perhaps the most complete of all the Gospels. It was a compilation the Holy Spirit brought through Dr. Luke after a careful verification and authentication of all the facts about the Lord Jesus from His birth through His ministry to His resurrection. In narrating the story of the Lord Jesus, we learn more about the nature and character of Doctor Luke himself.

DISCUSSION

I. HE GENERALLY SHOWS INTEREST IN PEOPLE (Luke 1:5-25; 10:38-42)

II. HE ALSO GIVES ATTENTION TO SOCIALLY INSIGNIFICANT PERSONS
(Luke 19:1-10)

III. HE GIVES STRONG ATTENTION TO PRAYER (Luke 11:1-4, 5-10; 18:10-14)

IV. HE ALSO EMPHASIZES ON JOY AND PRAISE (Luke 1:68-79; 1:46-55)

V. HE SHOWS INTEREST IN WOMEN PERSONALITIES (Luke 2:36-38; 7:11-15)

VI. HE SHOWS INTEREST IN THE HOLY SPIRIT'S PRESENCE (Luke 3:21, 22; 11:13)

VII. HE GIVES SPECIAL ATTENTION TO GENTILES AS THE LESS PRIVILEGED (Luke 2:32; 24:47)

VIII. HIS USE OF MEDICAL TERMS BETRAYS HIM AS A PHYSICIAN

(Luke 4:38; 5:12)

CONCLUSION

Doctor Luke wrote his gospel as a doctor and intellectual only after careful research. But he also wrote as a concerned missionary and gave attention to all the shades of people who needed attention like women, children and so on. He also did not neglect the more important spiritual issues like prayer and the Holy Spirit. Thanks be to the Lord Jesus for bringing men like Doctor Luke into His ministry as faithful supporters and co-workers.

4

Text: Luke 24:47

Theme: Additional Character Qualities of Luke as a Christian

INTRODUCTION

Doctor Luke as a Christian has so many good characteristics which cannot be overlooked in any of the discussions of his character. Though this has already been done partially in some of the sermons discussed, we want to complete this discussion in this sermon to help us to walk aright as Christians who are also faced with some of the challenges Doctor Luke also meet both in the exercise of his profession and in his work as a missionary of the Lord Jesus Christ. Some of these qualities are as follows:

DISCUSSION

I.   HE WAS PROBABLY A GREEK CHRISTIAN
  1. Luke was a Greek Christian. Proof of this can be deduced from his intellectual and literacy background. He had an outstanding command of the Greek language. **His vocabulary was wide-ranging and rich, and his style at times approached that of classical Greek.** (Luke 1:1-4)

II. HE WAS A MAN WHO WAS WELL CULTURED
  1. He addressed his two books politely to a high official he called Theophilus. (Luke 1:3-4; Acts 1:1,2)

III. HE WAS A MAN WHO WAS SYMPATHETIC (Luke 8:1-3)

IV. HE WAS A MAN WHO WAS VERY SPIRITUAL (Luke 1:35; 3:16)

V.   HE WAS A QUALIFIED PHYSICIAN (Colossians 4:14)

VI. HE WORKED WITH PAUL ON HIS PEREGRINATIONS (Acts 16:11-12)

CONCLUSION

Doctor Luke had these additional excellent qualities to make him capable of living as a serious Christian who in addition qualified to be used by the Lord Jesus Christ in the furtherance of the Gospel. In this, his credibility rating is very high. Thanks be to God that the Holy Spirit brought him just at the right time as a worthy instrument in the propagation of the gospel.

MATTHIAS

1

Text: Acts 1:26

Theme: Some Challenges from the life of Apostle Matthias

INTRODUCTION

Apostle Matthias came into the ministry as a replacement for Judas Iscariot who died a tragic and shameful death after betraying Jesus. When this happened and the disciples gathered in the upper room after the resurrection, Peter rightly stood before them and encouraged them to choose a successor to Judas to meet the number of disciples initially chosen by Christ. In Christ's estimation, He chose twelve would-be Apostles and this number had to be maintained after the death of Judas. We can also learn some good things from him as follows:

DISCUSSION
I.   IT IS BELIEVED THAT HE WAS ONE OF THE SEVENTY SENT BY CHRIST. (Luke 10:9, Luke 10:17)
II. HE WAS A WITNESS TO THE RESURRECTION OF CHRIST (Acts 1:22)
III. HE MAINTAINED PERSEVERANCE (Acts 1:21)
IV. HE MAINTAINED THE LIFE OF PURITY (Acts 1:24)
V. HE BOLDLY ACCEPTED THE CHALLENGE AS AN APOSTOLIC PREACHER (Acts 1:25, 26)

CONCLUSION

The need to get ready and get prepared for the appearing of the Lord Jesus Christ all the time is always emphasized in the scriptures. But in addition to this, readiness to service in the Church of Christ must also be maintained all the time so that anytime the Lord Jesus needs us, we shall be available. Matthias passed this test and became a faithful Apostle of Christ before and after Pentecost.

2
Text: Luke 10:17
Theme: A Brief life story of Apostle Matthias

INTRODUCTION
When Judas betrayed the Lord Jesus for 30 pieces of silver, it did not change what God had planned to get the church of Christ started. It also did not change the coming of the Holy Spirit as promised by Christ. But since there was the need for his replacement for the college of Apostles to still remain at twelve, Matthias was chosen by lot to replace him. His brief life story goes as follows:

DISCUSSION
I.   IT IS BELIEVED THAT MATTHIAS WAS ONE OF THE 72 DISCIPLES SENT BY CHRIST
(Luke 10:17)
II. MATTHIAS WAS CHOSEN TO REPLACE JUDAS WHO BETRAYED CHRIST
(Acts 1:26)
III. ACCORDING TO GREEK TRADITION, MATTHIAS PREACHED THE GOSPEL IN CAPPADOCIA
IV. TRADITION SAYS MATTHIAS DIED FOR THE COURSE OF CHRIST
    1. Tradition says that Matthias died as a martyr in modern day Ethiopia after being stoned and beheaded.

CONCLUSION
Matthias' short ministry and his end in life draw our attention to what 1 Corinthians 15:58 says in the words: "Therefore, my

beloved brethren, be steadfast, immovable, always abounding in the work of the Lord, knowing that your labor is not in vain in the Lord." NKJV. Though Matthias' ministry did not span a long period, it is certain his labour will never be in vain as stated in this verse.

MARK

1
Text: Philemon 1:23 with 24a
Theme: Knowing the Identity of John Mark

INTRODUCTION

John Mark was a young man by the time Jesus was arrested and crucified. He was associated with both Apostle Peter and Apostle Paul. Though the story of his life is very brief, he is a significant character because of some of the major things he allowed God to use him to do. Let us find out who he was from this sermon.

DISCUSSION
I.   HIS NAME WAS JOHN MARK
     (2 Timothy 4:11; Philemon 24; 1 Peter 5:13)
II. HE WAS BORN AS THE SON OF MARY
     (ACTS 12:12)
III. JOHN MARK BECAME A COMPANION OF PAUL AND BARNABAS IN MINISTRY
     (Acts 12:25)
IV. JOHN MARK WAS THE COUSIN OF BARNABAS IN PARENTAGE
     (COLOSSIANS 4:10)

V. JOHN MARK BECAME THE INTERPRETER OF APOSTLE PETER AND WROTE DOWN THE GOSPEL OF MARK AS DICTATED BY PETER

1. Papias confirms John Mark as the writer of the Second Gospel. Irenaeus (A.D. 130-200), **Bishop of Lugdunum (Lyon), Apologist, and leading Christian theologian of the 2nd century** also writes, "After their departure, Mark, the disciple and interpreter of Peter, did also hand down to us in writing what had been preached by Peter."

VI. A CONFLICT AROSE OVER HIM DURING PAUL'S SECOND MISSIONARY JOURNEY (ACTS 15:36-40)

VII. JOHN MARK IS BELIEVED TO BE THE YOUNG MAN WHO FLED DURING THE ARREST OF JESUS (Mark 14:51-52)

CONCLUSION

Though there are a few controversies about who John Mark really was in the New Testament, all the interpreters at least agree on the 7 major issues mentioned about him in this sermon. In spite of these controversies, he was useful to the Lord in many ways. What about you? What can we also do today to help build God's kingdom as John Mark did?

MATTHEW

1

Text: Matthew 9:9-13

Theme: The Calling of Apostle Matthew

INTRODUCTION

Matthew was called by Christ like all the other disciples who later became His Apostles. The story of his call is very important and dramatic because it is one of the most challenging among all those called by Jesus. It has some of the following details:

DISCUSSION

I. MATTHEW'S NAME WAS SIGNIFICANT
    1. It means "gift of Jehovah," or "gift of God."
    2. Matthew also bore the name Levi which could have been the real name given to him at birth or a nickname. (Mark 2:13-17; Luke 5:27-28)
    3. The name Levi could also have been a tribal designation meaning he was from the tribe of Levi. (Acts 2:14)

II. MATTHEW'S BUSINESS WAS SHAMEFUL
    1. Matthew was a well-known tax collector. (Mark 2:14; Matthew 9:9)
    2. Though this business was lucrative, it was despised by the Jews because it involved a lot of cheating and stealing coming from overcharging. Consequently, tax collectors

were regarded as sinners by the Jews. (Matthew 9:11; Mark 2:16)

3. Matthew later invited Jesus to a banquet of many tax collectors. (Mark 2:15)

III. MATTHEW'S CALL WAS SUDDEN

1. When he was invited by Christ, he followed him to become one of His twelve disciples. (Matthew 9:9: Mark 2:14)

2. Thereafter, he became one of the most trusted disciples of Christ Jesus whose name is mentioned in every list of the disciples. (Matthew 10:2-4; Luke 6:13-16)

IV. MATTHEW BECAME A SCRIPT WRITER

1. As a disciple, he walked with Jesus and became acquainted with all His teachings, miracles, healings, death and resurrection which he wrote down as the Gospel of Matthew. There are internal biblical proofs that Matthew wrote down the gospel which bears his name. Some of them can be quoted as follows:

2. "After Jesus called Matthew to become his disciple, he organized a dinner in his house to which he invited Jesus. In writing the account of this episode, Matthew chapter 9:10 indicates that the dinner was held "in the house" (KJV). When Mark recorded the same account in Mark chapter 2:15, he wrote that the dinner took place 'in his house' (KJV)."

3. "Matthew mentioned figures in the accounts of the gospel which only someone conversant with figures could have provided. In Matthew chapter 26:15, only Matthew recorded the exact amount (thirty shekels of silver) Judas Iscariot was paid for betraying Jesus and when Judas

returned the blood money, he also recorded thirty shekels of silver as in Matthew chapter 27:3. Naturally, only a tax collector who is used to figures would be recording such values with the exactitude that is seen in the gospel of Matthew, hence, a proof that he wrote the gospel."

V. MATTHEW'S LIFE AND MINISTRY ENDED IN SUCCESS
1. Tradition says that after the death and resurrection of Christ, he preached in Ethiopia.
2. Tradition also says that he died in Ethiopia as a martyr.

CONCLUSION

If we do not remember anything about Matthew and his ministry for the Lord Jesus Christ, the presence of the Gospel of Matthew in the list of the 27 New Testament Books is a big testimony which proves that Matthew's sacrifice to become a follower and disciple of the Lord Jesus Christ was worthwhile. For how many years have Matthew being preaching through this Gospel up till today. Christ surely had a purpose for him and when he sacrificed all his wealth to be able to respond to this call, God left a great legacy for the church through him.

2

Text: Luke 5:29

Theme: Some Spiritual lessons we can learn from the life of Apostle Matthew

INTRODUCTION

Matthew the Apostle is an important character in the New Testament whose nature and activities offer several important spiritual challenges. The steps he took to follow Christ involved great sacrifices, boldness and defiance of social prejudice. Some of the details of his life can be discussed in this sermon as follows:

DISCUSSION

I.   MATTHEW'S OTHER NAME WAS ALSO SIGNIFICANT
    1. His father's name was Alphaeus. (Mark 2:14)
    2. Before his call, he was called Levi. (Mark 2:14)
    3. Nobody knows why his name became Matthew which is the short form of the name Mattathias.
    4. The name Matthew means ""gift of Yahweh" or simply "the gift of God."

II. MATTHEW MOVED FROM A CROOKED SINNER TO BECOME A TRANSFORMED SAINT
    2. He began as tax collector, one of the most sinful professions of his day. **(Matthew 9:11; Mark 2:16)**
    3. Traditions says, Matthew preached for 15 years after the death of Christ before going out of Jerusalem as an international missionary.
    4. Tradition says Matthew ended up as a martyr in Ethiopia.

III. MATTHEW PAID A GREAT PRICE FOR HIS SALVATION

1. When called by Christ, he abandoned his lucrative business and the pleasures of this world to be able to respond to God's call (Matthew 9:9-13)

IV. MATTHEW WAS A LOYAL DISCIPLE WHO NEVER RETURNED TO WHAT WAS SECULAR

1. The fact that he is mentioned together with the other disciples in the upper room proves this. (Acts 1:13)

CONCLUSION

Matthew was one disciple who will forever be remembered as a person who made a great sacrifice for his salvation by moving out of his wealth, social prominence and social wellbeing to be able to become a disciple of the Lord Jesus Christ. We should remember that when the Lord Jesus Christ called other businessmen like Matthew, they could not follow Him because they couldn't sacrifice their wealth. But when Matthew got the opportunity, he sacrificed everything to be able to take advantage of it.

3

Text: Acts 1:13

Theme: Matthew, the gift of God

INTRODUCTION

The name Matthew means the gift of God and truly he joined the fold of the disciples of Jesus as a true gift of God. His other name was Levi and as a rich man he worked at the customs to receive taxes. His life has some valuable lessons for us three of which can be discussed in this sermon as follows:

DISCUSSION

I. MATTHEW DID HIS BEST TO MAKE A GREAT SACRIFICE (Matthew 9:9a; Mark 2:14a)

II. MATTHEW DEFIED ALL THE ODDS TO BECOME A FAITHFUL DISCIPLE OF HIS SAVIOUR (Mark 2:14b; Matthew 9:9b; Luke 5:27-28)

III. MATTHEW HAD AN OPEN-MINDED AND TEACHABLE SPIRIT
(Luke 5:29-31; Acts 1:13, 14)

CONCLUSION

If there is one person whose sacrifice is great and whose life is admirable among the disciples of Jesus, it is Matthew. The type of work he was doing classified him among the richest people of his day. But he placed his salvation after meeting Jesus over and above all other considerations. Is he not a special gift from God then as his name depicts? How many rich people of his status today and at the time he lived will be prepared to sacrifice their wealth to do what he did?

PETER

1
Text: Matthew 19:27 with John 21:7
Theme: The Call and Nature of Apostle Peter

INTRODUCTION

Apostle Peter was also one of the called disciples of Jesus Christ. He was one of the first to be called. In fact, he and his brother Andrew were the first set of disciples called by the Lord Jesus Christ. Though Peter was called as an ordinary unschooled fisherman, he exercised a very important ministry in the overall plan of God for the Church. His life proves that God needs our availability before our abilities can come in. We want to look at Apostle Peter's call and some of his dominant character qualities in this sermon.

DISCUSSION

I. APOSTLE PETER CAME TO JESUS WITH HIS NAME SIMON WHICH MEANS HEARING
   1. He came to Jesus with the name Simon which means "hearing."
   2. Jesus also gave him the name Peter which means "stone" or "rock." (John 1:42)

II. APOSTLE PETER CAME TO JESUS BECAUSE OF WHAT HE HEARD

1. Peter was a fisherman in Capernaum, beside the sea of Galilee. (Matthew 4:18-20)
2. Jesus selected several of His disciples here including Peter. (Matthew 4:18-20, 10:2; 16:16-19)
3. He was exercising his normal profession as a fisherman together with his brother Andrew when Jesus called them to follow Him. (Matthew 19:27)
4. After his call, Apostle Peter grew to become the most prominent of all the disciples who delivered a great message on the Day of Pentecost. (Acts 2:14-41)
5. He was the first disciple to acknowledge the divinity of Jesus after confessing Him to be the Messiah and the Son of God. (Matthew 16:15, 16)

III. APOSTLE PETER CAME TO JESUS WITH A SPECIAL NATURE AND HEART
1. Apostle Peter came to Jesus with an impulsive nature which is a nature which often acts quickly and hastily without forethought. (Matthew 16:21-23; 26:31-35, 69-75)
2. Proof of Apostle Peter's impulsive nature can be found in the following episodes:
   a. He quickly brought an inappropriate suggestion during the time of Christ's transfiguration. (Matthew 17:4)
   b. He hastily objects to having his feet washed by Christ at the Last Supper. (John 13:8)
   c. He cuts off the ear of Malchus during the arrest of Jesus. (John 18:10, 11)
   d. He quickly leaps out of the fishing boat to swim to the risen Christ who is standing on the shore. (John 21:7)

IV. APOSTLE PETER WAS RESPECTFUL, TENDER-HEARTED
AND HUMBLE
1. He shows this in his objection to Jesus washing his feet in
his impulsiveness which is a good expression of this good
nature. (John 13:1-9)

CONCLUSION

Apostle Peter, sometimes called "Peter the Great" by several
preachers started well with Jesus by responding quickly to His
call but also came with his nature and character as "Peter the
Great". His impulsiveness is well known as well as his self-
confidence and over enthusiasm. But he remained faithful to his
Lord and fulfilled his call to His glory. Let us always think of
being available to the Lord Jesus first. He alone knows how to
mould us so that our abilities can be channelled to proper use.

2

Text: Matthew 26:75

Theme: Some important Spiritual Lessons from the Life of Apostle Peter

INTRODUCTION

A lot of people are only interested in talking about the impulsiveness of Apostle Peter without looking at his other positive qualities which enabled the Lord Jesus Christ to use him mightily in the history of the Church. In this sermon, we want to look at some of these good and beneficial qualities of Apostle Peter as examples we can also follow today. They include the following:

DISCUSSION

I. APOSTLE PETER HAD BOTH A REMORSEFUL AND REPENTANT SPIRIT WHICH PLEASED JESUS

1. He showed remorse when he heard the crowing of the cock. (Matthew 26:75)

2. He showed genuine repentance when he came back to Jesus with a broken and contrite heart after denying Him three times. (Psalm 34:18) (Matthew 26:75; Luke 24:12) (John 20:2-10)

II. APOSTLE PETER NEVER TOOK HIS WILL FROM THE LORD JESUS

1. After the crucifixion, some of the disciples joined Peter to go to sea. (John 21:2-3a)

2. After toiling the whole night without catching anything, they decided to come back to shore. (John 21:3b-4)

3. There, they obeyed the instruction of Jesus to cast their net without knowing He was the one. (John 21:4-6a)
4. After catching a large quantity of fish, Jesus revealed Himself to them. (John 21:6b-14)
5. After Jesus had subjected Peter to a test of time, Peter once again surrendered his will totally to his master. (John 21:15-17) (1 John 4:19)

III. APOSTLE PETER BECAME A BOLD WITNESS OF THE LORD JESUS

1. On the Day of Pentecost, Peter and the disciples received power from on high. (Acts 2:1-12)
2. When they were later brought before the Sanhedrin for teaching in the name of Jesus,
3. Peter was bold enough to tell this Jewish counsel about their complicity of the Lord Jesus Christ and their desire to continue to preach in the name of Jesus without any fear. (Acts 4:17-21)
4. Apostle Peter who denied Jesus is now able to stand boldly before this Jewish Council to insist on proclaiming Jesus. (Acts 4:19, 20)
5. This display of boldness by Peter is a good example to copy in the work of Christ. (Acts 2:8) (Ephesians 5:18; 2 Timothy 2:15)

CONCLUSION

Apostle Peter's picture of remorse and repentance which got him restored back to Jesus are good examples worth following. His refusal to take back his will into his own hands and refusal to go back to his old profession of fishing after meeting the resurrected Christ are also excellent lessons for all faithful Christian workers.

His boldness to face the Sanhedrin and his insistence on preaching the Gospel in spite of their threats and persecutions are worthy examples of sincere workers of Christ today. So Apostle Peter had his good and positive side which was highly commendable!

3

Text: Matthew 14:28

Theme: A Summary outline of the Life and Ministry of Apostle Peter

INTRODUCTION

While thanking God for the life of great men like Apostle Peter, we must also be ready to study their lives closely to learn lessons from how they performed their duties for God and further take caution from where they faulted so that we shall not repeat their mistakes in our contemporary ministries. Apostle Peter is one of the great apostles whose life story can be of great help in this regard. In light of this, we want to look at the summary of Apostle Peter's life and ministry in this sermon. It presents us with the following outline:

DISCUSSION
I.   APOSTLE PETER RECEIVED A DIRECT CALL
   1. Peter was called like all the other disciples. (Matthew 4:18, 19)
   2. Peter was also called Simon. (Matthew 10:2)
II. APOSTLE PETER WAS A MAN OF COURAGE AND CONFIDENCE
   1. He could step on the sea and move toward Jesus. (Matthew 14:28)
III. APOSTLE PETER SAW JESUS AS THE CHRIST (Matthew 16:15-16)
IV. APOSTLE PETER EXHIBITED FALSE CONFIDENCE (Mark 14:31)

V. APOSTLE PETER WAS VERY IMPULSIVE AND OFTEN
   CAREFREE
   (John 18:10)
VI. APOSTLE PETER WAS SOMETIMES COLD AND
   CARELESS
   (John 18:17, 18)
VII. FINALLY APOSTLE PETER REPENTED AND WAS
   SPIRITUALLY CURED
   (Mark 14:72)

CONCLUSION

After looking at some of the salient episodes in the life and career
of Apostle Peter and comparing him to our current lives, what
are some of the noticeable parallels and differences? Christ called
him like He called all of us. He had his good side like confessing
Jesus as the Messiah and being able to walk on the sea for some
time. But he also had his weak side by being impulsive, denying
and rejecting Jesus due to fear. But in all these, he sought his
restoration through tears and never abandoned Christ, his
Messiah. Peter's life must be an encouragement to us in all
situations.

4

Text: 1 Peter 1:1 with 2 Peter 1:1

Theme: How Apostle Peter fulfilled his call and commission

INTRODUCTION

Probably the one and only thing most people remember about Apostle Peter is his denial of the Lord Jesus at His trial. But soon after Peter's restoration, he accepted the challenge of leadership in ministry and did one of the most remarkable jobs in practical ministry for the Lord Jesus Christ. Christ foreseeing his future value for the Church did not leave him to backslide but encouraged and brought him back into the fold and used him mightily to glorify His name as this sermon shows us as follows:

DISCUSSION
I.   APOSTLE PETER WAS PREPARED FOR HIS FUTURE MINISTRY
    1. He visited the tomb with the women. (Luke 24:12; John 20:2-6)
    2. Jesus encouraged him with a personal message. (Mark 16:7)
    3. Jesus further encouraged him with his appearance. (Luke 24:34; 1 Corinthians 15:4, 5)
    4. He was again encouraged with Christ's second appearance at the sea of Tiberias. (John 21:1, 2)
II. APOSTLE PETER WAS COMMISSIONED FOR HIS PRACTICAL MINISTRATION

1. Apostle Peter received a practical commission from Christ. (John 21:15-17)
2. Apostle Peter thereafter remained in Jerusalem with the other disciples as commanded by Christ. (Acts 1:12, 13)
3. He began his commission with the replacement of Judas with Matthias. (Acts 1:15-22)
4. He preached his first powerful sermon at Pentecost. (Acts 2:14-40)

III. APOSTLE PETER EXHIBITED THE FRUITS OF MINISTRY MENTORSHIP

1. He healed the impotent man at the entrance to the temple. (Acts 3:1-10)
2. He healed the sick just like Christ. (Acts 5:15)
3. He endured persecution just like Christ. (Acts 5:17-42) (Acts 12:3-19)
4. He visited Lydda and healed Aeneas. (Acts 9:32-34)
5. He raised Dorcas back to life. (Acts 9:36-43)
6. He advocated the preaching of the gospel to the Gentiles also. (Acts 11:1-18; 15:7-11)
7. He left a legacy for the church of Christ by writing two epistles and dictating the gospel of Mark to John Mark. (1 Peter 1:1; 2 Peter 1:1)

CONCLUSION

Looking at what Christ and the Holy Spirit used Apostle Peter to do in the early church, can't we say for sure that His ministry benefits after his restoration far outweighed his denial? Let this be a lesson for us all that when we falter once or twice, it does not mean that we have failed. Amen!

5

Text: Luke 12:41

Theme: Lessons from the Practical Training of Apostle Peter

INTRODUCTION

Whenever Christ calls anybody, He equips and trains him both spiritually and practically to make him up to the task he is called to execute. Apostle Peter was not an exception to this rule. Let us look at the details of this in his call and training in this sermon.

DISCUSSION

I.   APOSTLE PETER WAS A MAN WHO CAME TO CHRIST WITH A SINCERE ATTITUDE

    1. He was genuinely called by Christ. (Matthew 4:18-20; Mark 1:16-18)

II.   APOSTLE PETER WAS ALWAYS A MAN OF ACTION

    1. He answered Jesus hastily on the question of who touched Him from the crowd. (Luke 8:45, 46)

    2. He rebuked Jesus when He foretold His suffering and persecution from the religious leaders. (Matthew 16:21-23; Mark 8:31-33)

    3. He flatly refused to let Jesus wash his feet. (John 13:6-11)

III.   APOSTLE PETER WAS BOTH INQUISITIVE AND ACQUISITIVE

    1. He sought the interpretation of the parable of the steward. (Luke 12:41)

    2. He sought the interpretation of the law of forgiveness. (Matthew 18:21)

    3. He sought the interpretation of the law of defilement. (Matthew 15:15)

4. He sought the interpretation of the prophecy of Jesus concerning His second coming. (Mark 13:3, 4)
5. He called attention to the withered fig tree. (Mark 11:21)

CONCLUSION

Many Christians often chant, "I want God to use me," "I want Christ to use me," but they forget the truth that Christ does not use somebody who is empty-headed! What can such a person do to further the work of the kingdom? That is why He first equips all His chosen vessels. Do you want Christ to use you in any way in His Church? Then first learn to humble yourself under His mighty hand for Him to prepare and equip you.

6

Text: Matthew 16:22, 23

Theme: Learning precious Lessons from the good and bad sides of Apostle Peter

INTRODUCTION

There is no character in this sinful world who is hundred percent bad or hundred percent good. The Fall has affected us in many ways so we always exhibit both good and bad qualities in whatever we do. This explains why even though God used Apostle Peter mightily we still want to look at some of his positive and negative sides in this sermon as follow:

DISCUSSION
I.   HE WAS A MAN CALLED BY CHRIST
     1.   The Bible has a record of His call. (Luke 5:1-11)
II. HE WAS A MAN WHO MADE A GREAT CONFESSION AND SHOWED GREAT FAITH AND COURAGE
     1.   He confessed the Lord Jesus as the Christ. (Matthew 16:16-19; Mark 8:29; Luke 9:20; John 6:68, 69)
     2.   He miraculously caught the fish with a coin in its mouth. (Matthew 17:24-27)
     3.   He miraculously walked upon the water of the sea of Galilee. (Matthew 14:28-31)
III. HE WAS A MAN WHO ALMOST FELL INTO CONDEMNATION
     1.   He was presumptuous in rebuking Jesus. (Matthew 16:22, 23; Mark 8:32, 33)
     2.   He demanded that he, the disciples and Christ should stay on the mount of transfiguration contrary to the plan of

God. (Matthew 17:1-4; Mark 9:2-6; Luke 9:28-33; 2 Peter 1:16-18)

CONCLUSION

Perfection is an ideal God has set before all the sincere followers of Christ in the words of Matthew 5:48, which reads, "Therefore you shall be perfect, just as your Father in heaven is perfect." This does not mean that if you have not reached this state of absolute perfection you are useless and God cannot use you in any profitable way in the kingdom. Absolute perfection is the final ideal we are all seeking to attain. Let us continue to strive towards it. But when we see some deficiencies and imperfections in our lives, let us quickly run to 1 John 1:8, 9 which says, "If we claim to be without sin, we deceive ourselves and the truth is not in us. If we confess our sins, he is faithful and just and will forgive us our sins and purify us from all unrighteousness." NIV

7

Text: John 21:15-17

Theme: Some essential Facts we should all know about Apostle Peter

INTRODUCTION

The church of the Lord Jesus Christ today needs men like Apostle Peter and the earlier Apostles who will determine to follow the Lord Jesus Christ with their whole lives even up to the point of death. This is required in missionary work in hostile nations which are given to wrong forms of worship. Apostle Peter's life is a pattern for this. With all his natural tendencies and weaknesses as a normal human being, Apostle Peter's dedication to Christ was exemplary. Let us find evidence for this in this sermon.

DISCUSSION

I. APOSTLE PETER BEGAN LIFE AS AN ORDINARY FISHERMAN AND A DRIFT-NETTER (Matthew 4:18; John 21:3)

II. APOSTLE PETER'S NATURE AND CHARACTER STOOD OUT AMONG ALL THE DISCIPLES (Matthew 14:25-31) (John 21:15-17)

III. APOSTLE PETER EVENTUALLY EMERGED AS THE LEADER OF THE DISCIPLES (Acts 1:15-21; 2:14-36) (Galatians 1:18)

IV. APOSTLE PETER WAS NAMED BY CHRIST FOR HIS FUTURE MINSTRY (Matthew 16:18)

V. APOSTLE PETER DIED IN HIS DEDICATION AS A MARTYR

1. Peter died as a martyr for Christ by being crucified upside down.

2. St. Peter is believed to have died as a martyr for his faith. Although his death is not described in Scripture, numerous writers of the time (or shortly thereafter) described his death as having occurred in Rome during the reign of the emperor Nero in 64 CE. According to tradition, St. Peter was crucified upside down because he felt unworthy to die in the same manner as Jesus Christ. (Britannica.com)

CONCLUSION

Starting with Christ with your conversion and calling is very often not too difficult to do because it involves the exercise of your personal will without any undue external pressure from outside. But the major problem is being able to stay with Him all through your life until the time of your death. Between the time of your conversion and calling and the time of your death, there are so many things that can destroy your faith and commitment to Christ. So, blessed are you if you are able to finish your life still holding on to your faith and remaining firmly committed to Christ like Peter.

PAUL

1
Text: Acts 22:3
Theme: The Story of Paul's life until he met Christ

INTRODUCTION
The story of Paul's early life is an epitome of the grace of God in our conversion. His background and early activities completely alienated him from Christ. But this same gracious Jesus Christ took the initiative to go and meet him with his love, mercy and grace on the road to Damascus at a time he was on a mission of destruction. It was in this same way that the Lord Jesus Christ met all of us though the levels of grace differ from person to person. What were the details of Paul's life at this stage of his life? They are as follows:

DISCUSSION
I. PAUL WAS TRAINED AS A STRICT JEW
    1) His Jewish name was Saul. (Acts 8:1; 9:1; 13:9)
    2) He was of the tribe of Benjamin. (Romans 11:1; Philippians 3:5)
    3) His personal appearance was weak and contemptible. (2 Corinthians 10:1, 10)
    4) He was born in Tarsus. (Acts 9:11; 21:39; 22:3)
    5) He was educated in the school of Gamaliel. (Acts 22:3; 26:4)

6) He was a zealous Pharisee. (Acts 23:6; 26:5; 2 Corinthians 11:22; Galatians 1:14; Philippians 3:5, 6)
7) He was born as a Roman citizen. (Acts 16:37; 22:25-28)

II. PAUL BECAME AN ENEMY OF THE LORD JESUS

1) He persecuted the early Christians. (Acts 8:3; 9:1, 13, 14; 22:4, 19; Galatians 1:13; 1 Timothy 1:13)
2) He was present and gave consent to the stoning of Stephen. (Acts 7:58; 8:1; 22:20)
3) He was sent to Damascus with letters for the arrest of Christians and return them to Jerusalem. (Acts 9:1, 2)

III. PAUL WAS CONFRONTED BY THE LORD JESUS

1) Christ met him through a vision which led to his great conversion. (Acts 9:3-22; 22:4-19; 26:9-15; 1 Corinthians 9:1; 15:8; Galatians 1:16; 1 Timothy 1:12, 13)
2) He was immediately baptized after his conversion. (Acts 9:18; 22:16)
3) Thereafter, he was called to be an apostle of Christ. (Acts 22:14-21; 26:16-18; Romans 1:1; 1 Corinthians 1:1; 9:1, 2; 15:9; Galatians 1:1, 15, 16; Ephesians 1:1; Colossians 1:1; 1 Timothy 1:1; 2:7; 2 Timothy 1:1, 11; Titus 1:1, 3)

CONCLUSION

Whenever and wherever God's grace comes to us, the early life of Apostle Paul has taught us to humble ourselves and take advantage of it because such opportunities do not come repeatedly. Though Paul was a die-hard Pharisee, as soon as Christ showed him His grace on the road to Damascus, he turned round immediately, embraced the salvation of Christ and became

His follower. May we also constantly yield to the promptings of the Holy Spirit as Paul did.

2

Text: Acts 9:1-30

Theme: The Story of Paul's Conversion

INTRODUCTION

Paul's sudden and unexpected conversion was one of the most dramatic episodes in the history of the early church. As Paul himself mentions several times, he was a strong enemy of the infant Church of the Lord Jesus Christ who did his best to destroy it totally by organising attacks on the believers and finding occasion to accuse them so that they would either be killed or imprisoned. He was zealous in this great work for the devil until Christ Himself revealed His glory to him in his evil mission to Damascus. The details of Paul's conversion can be discussed in this sermon in the following details:

DISCUSSION

I. PAUL'S CONVERSION WAS SUDDEN (v. 3-9)
   1. It came when Christ revealed His glory. (Acts 9:3)
   2. It came when Christ spoke on authority. (Acts 9:4-7)
   3. It came when Paul became blind and had to be led to Damascus. (Acts 9:8-9)

II. PAUL'S CONVERSION CAME AS AN EVENT WHICH WAS SPECIAL (v. 12, 15)
   1. Christ showed him the purpose of this encounter. (Acts 9:15)
   2. Christ directed him to where he can get help. (Acts 9:12)

III. PAUL'S CONVERSION WAS SHOCKING (v. 13-14, 26-30)
   1. It was shocking to his collaborators. (Acts 9:13, 14)
   2. It was shocking to the believers. (Acts 9:26-30)

CONCLUSION

Paul's conversion and its aftermath was like a lion coming to stand behind a strongly fenced sheep pen and telling the sheep inside, "I have now become as gentle as you are so open me for brotherly fellowship." Which sheep will understand and take this to come and open the gates for the lion to come in? How can you be sure that what the lion is saying is true? In history, how many lions have turned to be as gentle as a sheep? This is a picture of the shock and surprise which greeted Paul's conversion on the road to Damascus. But it tells us that we can never be enemies of God and the gospel forever. One day, He will speak at a time we are not expecting Him to do this and His glory will be manifested through the omnipotent power which He will display.

3

Text: Acts 13:6-10

Theme: Some major episodes in Apostle Paul's Life and Ministry (I)

INTRODUCTION

When we avail ourselves to God in ministry, it becomes His responsibility to lead and guide us in the best possible ways to be able to fulfil our call. We have a very good example of this in Paul's ministry where He used some close and distant relatives to support him in his ministry to the Gentiles. Let us look at this in this sermon:

DISCUSSION

I. APOSTLE PAUL WAS CALLED AND PREPARED FOR HIS MINISTRY
    1. Paul didn't jump right into long-term ministry. (Galatians 1:13-18) (Galatians 1:17)

II. GOD USED PAUL'S NEPHEW TO SAVE HIS LIFE AND MINISTRY
    1. Paul's nephew saved his life. (Acts 23:16-24)

III. APOSTLE PAUL ALREADY HAD A DUAL NAME BEFORE HIS MINISTRY
    1. Saul's name was not changed to Paul (Acts 13:9)

CONCLUSION

We have examples of this in the Bible of God using some insignificant people to fulfil His great plans and purposes. He used a maid to bring healing to Naaman. He used the bread and fish of a lad to feed thousands. He also used Paul's nephew in this sermon to save his life and ministry. When God determines to work, because he is the omnipotent creator, He is able to use anything anywhere no matter how insignificant it is to fulfil His great plans and purposes. So let us take courage because when it comes to God making a way where there is no way, He can always do this by His great power.

4

Text: 2 Corinthians 1:8-11

Theme: Some major episodes in Apostle Paul's Life and Ministry (II)

INTRODUCTION

Christ's call is always a call to duty and the fulfilment of great responsibilities in the kingdom of God. So whenever it comes to us, we must bear this in mind and strengthen our hands in the power of the Holy Spirit to be good stewards and soldiers. Apostle Paul did this in his moment of stress and suffering in his ministry. We have an example of this in this sermon as follows:

DISCUSSION

I. ALL THE ABUNDANT RESPONSIBILITIES IN APOSTLE PAUL'S MINISTRY CAME FROM GOD
    1. Had it not been his total reliance on the Holy Spirit, it could be asserted that God gave Paul more than he could handle. (2 Corinthians 1:8-11)

II. WHEN APOSTLE PAUL NEEDED ENCOURAGEMENT, HE WAS CALLED TO HEAVEN BY GOD
    1. Paul visited heaven before his death. (2 Corinthians 12:1-10) (Galatians 1:17)

III. WHEN APOSTLE PAUL WAS DESERTED BY ALL, IT REMAINED ONLY GOD
    1. Paul felt deserted by everyone but God. (2 Timothy 4:9-18) (2 Corinthians 12:9) (2 Timothy 4:6-8)

CONCLUSION

When the Lord Jesus says in Matthew 28:20 that ""*... and lo, I am with you always, even to the end of the age." Amen."* NKJV, He means what He has said. Without His help, support and encouragement, nobody can be a successful minister or servant of His. He knew this that was why He told the disciples before leaving them to the task of global evangelization. This is what we witness in this sermon in the ministry of Apostle Paul. After God had given him His great task, He encouraged him when he needed encouragement and stood firmly behind him when all others deserted him. Faithful is our Lord!

5

Text: 2 Timothy 4:16

Theme: Some essential character qualities for ministry in God's Vineyard (I)

INTRODUCTION

The work of ministry makes several demands on the minister one of which is that, the mister is to live by what he preaches as an example to the congregation exactly as Christ did for the Church. We should never forget that whatever Christ taught His followers to do, He first did it as an example to them. To minister successfully, you need certain unavoidable character traits including the following we are going to discuss in this sermon as demonstrated in the life of Apostle Paul.

DISCUSSION

I.   APOSTLE PAUL WAS ALWAYS PERSISTENT
     (Philippians 3:13, 14)
II. APOSTLE PAUL ALWAYS MINISTERED IN PATIENCE
     (Acts 9:15; 22:15; 26:17) (Galatians 1:17; 2:1)
III. APOSTLE PAUL ALWAYS MINISTERED WITH FIRMNESS
     (Galatians 2:11, 13) (1 Corinthians 9:6) (2 Peter 3:15)
IV. APOSTLE PAUL WAS ALWAYS FORGIVING
     (2 Timothy 4:16)

CONCLUSION

As faithful ministers of Christ, we need persistence to be able to move on in difficulties. We also need patience to handle all the difficult people in the congregation. Firmness is also required to guide the people to the right path. A forgiving spirit is also necessary to help us forgive and continue to lead offending sinners. This is the only way we can do God's work successfully as ministers and shepherds.

6

Text: 1 Corinthians 9:19-23

Theme: Some essential character qualities for ministry in God's Vineyard (II)

INTRODUCTION

In God's kingdom into which all His genuine servants are called, certain ministry attitudes are required to maintain a healthy working relationship between Christ and all His workers. It is these attitudes which make ministry in God's vineyard both possible and practicable. Without these attitudes, pride and arrogance which led to the fall of the devil can come into the hearts of God's servants and lead to their fall as the work progresses and people start pouring forth praises for the great works God is doing. These attitudes are therefore essential for all workers as identified and discussed in Paul's life and ministry in this sermon as follows:

DISCUSSION

I. ALL TRUE SERVANTS OF GOD HAVE TO BE COURAGEOUS
(Acts 18:9) (Acts 13:4; 14:22)

II. ALL GENUINE SERVANTS OF GOD MUST BE CONCERNED
(Romans 12:17) (Philemon 18) (1 Corinthians 9:16-19)

III. ALL FAITHFUL SERVANTS OF GOD NEED TO BE HUMBLE
(Acts 15:1, 2) (2 Corinthians 11:5) (1 Corinthians 9:12)

IV. ALL FAITHFUL SERVANTS MUST BE HUMANE
(1 Corinthians 9:19-23; Acts 21:17-26)

CONCLUSION

To be able to die and give Himself as a ransom for many, the Lord Jesus exhibited all these characteristics mentioned in this sermon. His purpose was to live a pattern for all His future workers so that if they truly want to walk in His steps in ministry, they will get a perfect picture of how He wants them to walk as faithful servants. If the Lord Jesus Christ has left us these examples as servants, then we have no other choice than to portray these truths as Apostle Paul did his best to do throughout his ministry.

7

Text: Romans 5:3-4

Theme: Some important Spiritual Lessons from the life of Apostle Paul (I)

INTRODUCTION

Though God always appreciates and rewards what we do for Him, He is more interested in what we are than what we do for Him. We should remember that, in the end, Christ is going to tell some people who will appeal to what they did for entrance into His kingdom to get away from Him because in spite of all the signs and wonders they performed, lived and walked in iniquity. This is proof that though God is always interested in what we do for Him, He is more interested in what we are for Him. God could use Apostle Paul first because of who he was after his conversion on the road to Damascus. This is why we want to learn who Paul was in character in this sermon with the discussion of the following character traits:

DISCUSSION
I.   APOSTLE PAUL POSSESSED THE HEART OF A SERVANT (Acts 20:19)
II. APOSTLE PAUL ALWAYS MINISTERED BY BEING LED BY THE SPIRIT (Acts 20:22)
III. APOSTLE PAUL ALWAYS SERVED BY BEING FILLED BY THE SPIRIT (Acts 20:23)
IV. APOSTLE PAUL ALWAYS MINISTERED AS A FAITHFUL SHEPHERD (Acts 20:28, 37, 38)
V.   APOSTLE PAUL NURTURED UNDER-SHEPHERDS (Acts 20:28-29)

VI. APOSTLE PAUL ALWAYS MINISTERED AS A GOOD SOLDIER (Acts 20:31)

CONCLUSION

What we are is necessary to help us to do what we are supposed to do. That was why Christ never trained His Apostles like Paul only to preach the gospel and also perform signs and wonders but first and foremost strive forward towards perfection in character by telling them in Matthew 5:48, *"Therefore you shall be perfect, just as your Father in heaven is perfect."* NKJV. Let us all learn a great lesson from this as shepherds and ordinary workers of God.

8

Text: Romans 5:3-4

Theme: Some important Spiritual Lessons from the life of Apostle Paul (II)

INTRODUCTION

In training His disciples to be faithful future Apostles, Christ sometimes admonished them against what He called the leaven of the Pharisees. The leaven of the Pharisees in the broad sense includes the hypocrisy and all the other negative character defects of the Pharisees and the religious leaders which led them to reject the Messiah in spite of all their external demonstration of piety and so-called devotion to God. Such attitudes do not bring success in ministry. In place of this, Christ always want us to cultivate some of the following important positive character qualities which were exemplified by Apostle Paul throughout His ministry. The details can be gleaned in this sermon as follows:

DISCUSSION

I.   PAUL WORKED FOR CHRIST WITH COMMITMENT (Acts 20:20)

II. PAUL DID GOD'S WORK WITH GREAT COMPASSIONATE (Acts 20:21)

III. PAUL DID GOD'S WORK WITH GREAT FAITHFULNESS (Acts 20:24)

IV. PAUL MINSTERED FOR CHRIST WITH FEARLESSNESS (Acts 20:22)

V.   PAUL MINISTERED FOR CHRIST BY BEING FERVENT (Acts 20:27)

CONCLUSION

You can either minster to fail or minister to succeed depending on your nature and character in the ministry and the attitude of heart with which you are serving people. Apostle Paul ministered to succeed because he ministered in full recognition of the virtues discussed above. People who minister like Apostle Paul as mentioned above are bound to succeed and glorify God in their service because what we are able to do is often largely dictated by who we are and where we are standing. Never neglect character in ministry because it can make you a cheerful, cherished and successful servant.

9

Text: Romans 5:3-4

Theme: Some important Spiritual Lessons from the life of Apostle Paul (III)

INTRODUCTION

Why did the Lord Jesus Christ instruct His disciples to pick the tiny broken pieces of bread after feeding the four thousand and five thousand people? Apart from teaching them the need to avoid wastefulness, Christ also wanted to instil some positive character qualities in them which are important for the success of all servant leaders such as the following the Holy Spirit caused Apostle Paul to demonstrate in his ministry.

DISCUSSION

I. APOSTLE PAUL ALWAYS AVOIDED GREED
   (Acts 20:33)

II. APOSTLE PAUL ALWAYS WORKED WITH THE SPIRIT OF GIVING
   (Acts 20:35)

III. APOSTLE PAUL ALWAYS WORKED WITH DILIGENCE
   (Acts 20:34)

IV. APOSTLE PAUL ALWAYS WORKED WITH TOTAL DEDICATION
   (Acts 20:34)

V. APOSTLE PAUL ALWAYS WORKED BY GIVING ATTENTION TO PRAYER AND GENUINE SPIRITUAL DEVOTION
   (Acts 20:36)

CONCLUSION

Successful ministry to the diverse people God brings into the service of His faithful workers requires all these important characteristics discussed in this sermon. So knowing them and depending upon prayer which is one of these characteristics to be able to cultivate them practically in our lives is an important recipe for success in the service of Christ. No sincere worker of Christ wants to end like Judas or Demas. If you want to live above these characters, then God has offered us a remedy in this sermon.

10
Text: Romans 5:3-4
Theme: Some important Spiritual Lessons from the life of Apostle Paul (IV)

INTRODUCTION

We should understand as God's servants that whenever we are called into the ministry, we are called into one of the highest professions which demands that we work on people both spiritually and physically and also work to bring them both present benefits and future security of their souls in heaven through salvation. This task calls for certain pragmatic characteristics which can make us successful in this great service for God. Some of these characteristics were amply demonstrated by Apostle Paul in his ministry as we are going to discuss in this sermon. Though sometimes he was misunderstood by his critics and enemies, these positive character attitudes were also greatly responsible for the success of Apostle Paul as the servant of the Lord Jesus on his way to Damascus. Some of these qualities are as follows:

DISCUSSION

I.   APOSTLE PAUL ALWAYS SERVED WITH HUMILITY
     (Acts 20:19)
II. APOSTLE PAUL ALWAYS MINISTERED WITH BOLDNESS
     AND HONESTY
     (Acts 20:21)
III. APOSTLE PAUL ALWAYS MINISTERED AS A FAITHFUL
     WORKER
     (Acts 20:20)

IV. APOSTLE PAUL ALWAYS MINISTERED AS A DEDICATED VISIONARY AND WORKMAN (Acts 20:26, 27)

V. APOSTLE PAUL MINISTERED FOR CHRIST AS A WARRIOR
(Acts 20:30)

CONCLUSION

If the work of ministering to people for Christ brings them benefits both here and hereafter, then what level of seriousness should we attach to this work. Where should we position ourselves to do the best for Christ. What positive character qualities should we cultivate to enable us to do this work very well. The simple answer is that we should follow in the steps of Christ first and further learn more from Apostle Paul in this sermon.

11

Text: Acts 21:11-13
Theme: The Outstanding Attributes of Paul as Christ's Witness to the Gentiles

INTRODUCTION
When the Lord Jesus Christ met Apostle Paul on the road to Damascus and became converted to Christianity, the Lord Jesus Christ further showed him his call. He made him aware that he is being called as a special apostle to bring the message of salvation to the Gentiles. This was a special call which required special standards of character because it was both dangerous and unheard of among Jews who always regarded Gentiles as dogs. Many character standards were needed for this calling but we want to discuss four of them which Apostle Paul possessed which made him successful in this mission. They are as follows:

DISCUSSION
I.   APOSTLE PAUL NEEDED GREAT COURAGE
     (Acts 23:12-14) (Acts 24:1-9) (Acts 24:21-26; 26:32; 28:30-31)
     (Acts 27:22-25)
II. APOSTLE PAUL NEEDED TO SHOW GREAT CONCERN
     (Acts 21:19-26)
III. APOSTLE PAUL NEEDED TO ENDURE GREAT SUFFERING
     (Acts 21:27-36) (Acts 20:23) (Acts 22:22; 27:42, 43)
V.   APOSTLE PAUL NEEDED TO MAKE A LOT OF SACRIFICES
VI. Acts 21:17-26) (Acts 23:29-31; 28:7-9)

CONCLUSION

Have we been called by the Lord Jesus? What is your mission? What is your message? What are your methods? Then let Apostle Paul be your mentor for he was one Apostle who was given more than what he could do as an individual by the Lord Jesus Christ and he did it with all his mind, heart and strength until the Lord called him home.

12

Text: Acts 27:39-44

Theme: Apostle Paul on the Island of Malta

INTRODUCTION

Whatever God plans shall always come to pass in spite of the problems, impediments and challenges. It was God's plan that Paul's ministry would take him to Rome to testify about His grace in this city also and with all the problems that came, God took him there. But before they got to Rome, they had to land at the Island of Malta because of the destruction of their ship by a storm. The story of their being on this island and what God did there to glorify His name goes like this:

DISCUSSION

I. PAUL AND HIS COMPANIONS WERE SAVED BY GOD'S GRACE

(Acts 27:37-44)

II. GOD USED PAUL ON THE ISLAND TO SHOW HIS GREATNESS

(Acts 28:3-4, 7-9)

III. THE PEOPLE OF MALTA ALSO EXPRESSED THEIR GRATITUDE

(Acts 28:10)

CONCLUSION

When you are almost shipwrecked and you are saved by grace on an island like Malta, will you continue to preach the Gospel and testify about Christ? Yet Apostle Paul did this on this island. He preached the message of salvation; he healed and did all the normal things in ministry which he could do as an apostle. This is the life of a servant who said *"For to me, to live is Christ and to die is gain."* NIV (Philippians 1:21). What Paul did on this Island is a good example worth following by all genuine servants of God.

13
Text: Acts 28:16
Theme: Paul's life and Ministry in Rome

INTRODUCTION

To Apostle Paul, life in Rome when he finally arrived there was still life in ministry and not life in idleness and despair. Though he arrived there as a prisoner under guard, he did not allow this to prevent him from taking advantage of this opportunity to preach the Gospel and share the message of salvation and redemption. Let us look at some of his activities while in Rome in this sermon as follows:

DISCUSSION
I.   PAUL HAD HIS FREEDOM AS A PRISONER (Acts 28:16)
II. PAUL HAD HIS CHANCE AS A PREACHER (Acts 28:17-20, 23)
III. PAUL HAD HIS CHANCE TO MEET MANY PEOPLE (Acts 28:15, 23a)

CONCLUSION

Impediments are not impossibilities because they can always be overcome to enable us continue with what we are doing and move towards our goal. Impediments must always be regarded as temporary setbacks but not as permanent roadblocks. When we do God's work with this mindset, the Holy Spirit will always make a way for us to enable us continue to do God's work.

14

Text: Acts 14:20

Theme: The miracle of Apostle Paul's resuscitation

INTRODUCTION

Though Apostle Paul went through different forms of persecutions throughout His ministry, one of the most fatal was his being stoned to death at Lystra by the Jews. Christ told Ananias after his encounter with Paul on the road to Damascus that Paul was a vessel chosen to bring the good news to the Jews and in addition suffer many things for His name's sake. This episode at Lystra was one of the many things he had to suffer for Christ. It has the following details:

DISCUSSION

I.   APOSTLE PAUL WAS STONED TO DEATH BY THE JEWS
     (Acts 14:19)

II. APOSTLE PAUL WAS STONED TO DEATH OUT OF JEALOUSY
     (Acts 14:9-18)

III. BUT APOSTLE PAUL WAS RESUSCITATED BY THE MIGHTY POWER OF JESUS
     (Acts 14:20)

CONCLUSION

Our Jesus is the almighty Jesus Christ! He is the son of God and co-creator with God. Nothing he has not sanctioned can ever take place against any of His chosen vessels. Even when they are killed, He alone has absolute power over life and death so He can bring them back to life to complete the task He has given to them.

When Apostle Paul's time of death finally came, He took him home. But before this time, nobody could take his life through any of the difficult situations He went through. This is the omnipotent God with His omnipotent power at work! May His name be praised forever and ever. What should you do with this Jesus today?

15

Text: 2 Timothy 4:6-8

Theme: The noble character of Apostle Paul

INTRODUCTION

If Christ and the Holy Spirit used Apostle Paul mightily in the work of God, it was because He possessed some personal and ministry qualities which made this possible. Of the 27 books of the New Testament, the Holy Spirit used him to produce 13 of them. These are Romans, 1 and 2 Corinthians, Galatians, Ephesians, Philippians, Colossians, 1 and 2 Thessalonians, 1 and 2 Timothy, Titus, and Philemon. What were some of these personal and ministry qualities of this great apostle? Let us look at some of them in this sermon as follows:

DISCUSSION

I. PAUL HAD SOME GOOD PERSONAL QUALITIES

1) He was courageous. (Acts 9:29; 20:22-24; 21:13; Ephesians 6:20; 1 Thessalonians 2:2)

2) He was bold even in facing death. (2 Timothy 4:6-8)

3) He was indomitable. (Romans 8:35-37; 1 Corinthians 4:9-13; 2 Corinthians 4:8-12; 6:4-10; 11:23-33; 12:10; 1 Thessalonians 2:2; 2 Timothy 1:12; 3:11; 4:17)

4) He was meek. (1 Corinthians 4:12, 13; 2 Timothy 4:16)

5) He was tactful. (1 Corinthians 9:19-22; 10:33; Philemon 7-14)

6) He was zealous. (Romans 9:3; 2 Corinthians 5:11-14; 6:4-10; 12:14, 15; Philippians 3:6-16; Colossians 1:29)

II. PAUL HAD SOME EXCELLENT MINISTRY QUALIFICATIONS
   1) He was purposeful in his work. (Acts 20:22, 23; 21:4, 10-14)
   2) He rejoiced in his sufferings and remained cheerful in adversity. (Philippians 2:17; Colossians 1:24; 2 Timothy 2:9) (1 Corinthians 4:9, 11-13) (Acts 16:25; Romans 8:35-37; 2 Corinthians 4:8-10; 12:10; 2 Timothy 2:10; 3:11, 12; 4:16, 17)
   3) He was self-supporting. (Acts 18:3; 20:33-35; 2 Corinthians 11:7, 9; 1 Thessalonians 2:9; 2 Thessalonians 3:8)

CONCLUSION

The ministry of the Lord Jesus Christ in the Church did not end when God called Apostle Paul home. The work of God has always been going on since that time. This means that God still needs some more 'Apostle Pauls' in today's ministry but where are they? Can't you be one of them after going through this sermon?

PHILEMON

1

Text: Philemon 1:5, 7

Theme: Some essential Character qualities of Philemon worth Copying (I)

INTRODUCTION

Philemon's name means loving and loving was exactly what Apostle Paul encouraged him to show towards Onesimus, his runaway slave as a fellow believer. Though this was very radical and unexpected in the society they were living at that time, Philemon was encouraged to do this to reveal a noble character which has the following character essentials.

DISCUSSION

I.   PHILEMON WAS A MAN OF ENCOURAGEMENT
     (Philemon 1:5, 7)

II. IN CHRIST, PHILEMON HAD TO UNDERSTAND EQUALITY
     (Philemon 1:15-17) (Galatians 3:28)

III. IN RELATIONSHIPS, PHILEMON HAD TO BE A MAN OF GOOD EXAMPLE
     (Philemon 1:10, 15-16)

IV. IN CHRIST, PHILEMON HAD TO UNDERSTAND PRAYER
     (Philemon 1:4-6)

V. IN CHRIST, PHILEMON HAD TO BECOME A PEACEMAKER
(Philippians 4:2-3) (Romans 12:18)

CONCLUSION

In Philemon's day, slaves had no social respect and occupied the lowest step of the social ladder. So for Onesimus to show disrespect to Philemon and further run away from him was an unforgivable social crime and misdemeanour. Yet Apostle Paul encouraged him to forget all these and accept Onesimus back as a fellow brother. If Philemon could do this, then he was a true Christian who was genuinely converted. Have you made any great sacrifice for your faith in Christ before. Then let the example of Philemon encourage you.

2

Text: Philemon 1:8-10

Theme: Some essential Character qualities of Philemon worth Copying (II)

INTRODUCTION
There are some additional lessons we can learn from the story of Philemon which is full of radical and revolutionary teachings. The story of Philemon teaches us spiritual equality within acceptable social norms and practices. Consequently, as it encourages masters and lords to do their part as Christians, it also encourages slaves and servants to fulfil their social roles within acceptable Christian principles of respect. These additional principles we can learn from this sermon are as follows:

DISCUSSION
I.   PEACEFUL CO-EXISTENCE DEMANDS FORGIVENESS
     (Philemon 1:17-19)
II. PEACEFUL CO-EXISTENCE DEMANDS THE SHOW OF FAVOUR
     (Philemon 1:14)
III. PEACEFUL CO-EXISTENCE DEMANDS THE SHOW OF FERVOUR
     (Hebrews 3:13; 1 Corinthians 5:12; 1 Thessalonians 5:14)
IV. PEACEFUL CO-EXISTENCE DEMANS THE SHOW OF PRACTICAL FORTITUDE
     (Philemon 1:10-13)

VI. PEACEFUL CO-EXISTENCE DEMANDS SERVICE IN FAITHFULNESS
(Philemon 1:8-10)

CONCLUSION

Paul taught Onesimus who was formerly not useful to Philemon as a runaway slave to bear practical fruits of genuine repentance and return to his master Philemon to serve him faithfully as the societal laws at that time demanded and dictated. In this, he was both teaching Philemon and Onesimus peaceful co-existence within the family and household of God. We all need to learn the truths outlined in this sermon and apply them daily to promote peace and good working relationships in the church of Christ. May we be good examples to each other in the great family of God.

PHILLIP

1

Text: John 1:43

Theme: Good and precious lessons we can learn from Phillip the Apostle

INTRODUCTION

Apostle Phillip is one servant whose life story and ministry offer some of the most powerful lessons we can learn in the Church of our Lord Jesus Christ today. Though his ministry is very brief as compared to people like Peter and Paul, his life lessons are spiritually some of the best we can ever have among the Apostles. Some of the prominent issues in his life include the following:

DISCUSSION

I. PHILLIP ANSWERED WHEN GOD CALLED
(John 1:43-44) (John 6:44)

II. PHILLIP BROUGHT OTHERS WHEN HE WAS CALLED
(John 1:45-46) (Matthew 11:21; Luke 10:13)

III. PHILLIP BROUGHT HOPE AND ASSURANCE THROUGH HIS CALLING
(John 1:46, 49)

IV. PHILLIP PASSED WHEN HE WAS TESTED BY CHRIST
(John 6:5-7; James 1:2-4; I Peter 1:6-8)

V. PHILLIP DEMONSTRATES THE NEED FOR A CLOSE RELATIONSHIP WITH CHRIST

(John 14:7-11) (John 14:6)

CONCLUSION

Phillip's encounter with Christ in the Gospels offer us several challenges today. First, it teaches us that we must answer anytime God calls us. Secondly, his life shows us the need to share the Good News with others. Thirdly, his life shows us the need to exercise faith in difficult situations. Finally, his life shows us the importance of drawing close to Christ to be able to learn from Him all the time. Let us note the precious lessons from Phillip in this sermon.

2

Text: Matthew 10:3 with Acts 1:13

Theme: All the Essentials we need to know about Phillip the Apostle I (His Early Life)

INTRODUCTION

Whoever Christ called in the early stages of His ministry, He called him for a special purpose to fulfil a special need. Apostle Phillip was no exception. As soon as he accepted Christ's invitation to be His disciple, God started manifesting His real purpose for calling him in his life. This was true soon after his call and later in his ministry. Let us look at the facts on this at the initial stage of his calling in this sermon with the following details:

DISCUSSION

I.   HIS NAME HAD A MEANING

   1.   His name means "Lover of horses."

II. HE WAS CALLED AS A MINISTER

   1.   He was called as an Apostle. (John 1:43-44)

III. HE WAS BORN IN GALILEE AS GOD'S FUTURE MESSENGER

   1.   He was probably born in the Galilean city of Bethsaida. (John 1:44)

IV. THROUGH NATHANIEL, HE IMMEDIATELY BEGAN HIS MINISTRY

(John 1:45, 46)

CONCLUSION

Phillip's early life and encounter with Christ reveal that when Christ called him, he understood his calling as service to God and started working immediately. Whenever God extends His hand to us like He did to Phillip, we should always act like this great disciple and yield all our members to Him not only to fulfil His purpose for calling us but also to glorify His name. The reason is that the fields are already white for harvest as John 4:35 says in the words: *"Do you not say, 'There are still four months and then comes the harvest'? Behold, I say to you, lift up your eyes and look at the fields, for they are already white for harvest!"* NKJV

3

Text: Acts 8:40

Theme: All the Essentials we need to know about Phillip the Apostle II (His Latter life)

INTRODUCTION

Phillip's latter life is filled with important lessons like his early life. It is important because although it still reveals his commitment to ministry, it talks about his ministry at a much higher level to further the work of the kingdom. It has very interesting ministry miracles such as the following we are going to discuss in this sermon as follows:

DISCUSSION
I.   PHILLIP SERVED AS A DEACON IN THE COURSE OF HIS MINISTRY (Acts 6:5)
II. PHILLIP WORKED AS AN EVANGELIST IN THE COURSE OF HIS MINISTRY (Acts 8:26, 40)
III. EVEN IN PERSECUTION, PHILLIP STILL MINISTERED (Acts 8:3-5)
IV. PHILLIP MINSTERED AS AN EVANGELIST IN SAMARIA (Acts 8:5)
V.   PHILLIP MINISTERED TO THE ETHIOPIAN EUNUCH WITH SUCCESS (Acts 8:26-38)
VI. THEREAFTER, PHILLP WAS CAUGHT AWAY BY THE SPIRIT (Acts 8:39)
VII. PHILLIP WENT TO AZOTUS TO CONTINUE HIS FAITHFUL SERVICE (Acts 8:40)
VIII. PHILLIP FINALLY ENDED UP IN CAESAREA STILL IN FAITHFUL SERVICE (Acts 8:40)

CONCLUSION

Servanthood and service are inseparable both in the spiritual and physical sense. Whenever we come to understand our servants of God, servants to the church of Christ and servants to the people of God, service becomes natural and joyful because we know we are working to fulfil a divine purpose. This was what led Jesus Christ to say in John 4:34 in the words: *"Jesus said to them, "My food is to do the will of Him who sent Me, and to finish His work.""* NKJV. Apostle Phillip's life was full of service from the day he was called until the end of his life. What a big challenge to us today.

SILAS

1
Text: Acts 15:22
Theme: God's message to us through Silas

INTRODUCTION

God has different ways of speaking to His people. He can speak through the Word. He can speak through personal convictions. He can speak in an audible voice as He spoke to Paul on his way to Damascus. He can also speak indirectly through personalities like Silas who are fully devoted and committed to Him. What is God's message to us through the life and ministry of Silas. Let us try to discover this in this sermon as follows:

DISCUSSION

I. WE MUST ALWAYS BE CHOSEN BY GOD FOR HIS GLORY
(Acts 15:22, 40-41) (Matthew 25:23)

II. GOD'S CHOICE CAN LEAD TO IMPRISONMENT BECAUSE OF HIS GLORY
(Acts 16:19-24) (Acts 5:41)

III. WHEN WE REJOICE IN OUR SUFFERING, GOD MANIFESTS HIS GLORY
(Acts 16:25-39) (Philippians 4:4)

IV. WE MUST ALWAYS BE SUPPORTIVE TO SEE GOD'S GLORY
(Acts 17:4-7) (1 Peter 1:22)

V. WE MUST LEARN TO BE FEARLESS TO BE USED TO
GLORIFY GOD

(Acts 17:10-15) (Isaiah 12:2)

VI. WE MUST WALK IN FAITHFULNESS TO BRING GLORY
TO GOD

(Acts 18:5) (Luke 16:11)

VII. WE MUST WALK AS PREACHERS CALLED FOR
GOD'S GLORY

(2 Corinthians 1:19; Acts 15:32) (2 Corinthians 4:5)

CONCLUSION

Being used to glorify God is always important and necessary for us as Christians and Christian workers. But this cannot happen in a vacuum. It always requires a good spiritual and practical disposition for this to happen such as are discussed in this sermon like faithfulness, fearlessness, faithful preaching, supportiveness and joy. This is God's message from Silas to us today.

2
Text: Acts 16:37 with Acts 15:40-41
Theme: The Background and Ministry of Silas

INTRODUCTION
There are some Christian workers in the New Testament like Silas who are certainly going to receive great rewards for what they went through adversity to be able to do even though they were not Apostles. Silas was a faithful and fearless worker of Christ who did his best for the kingdom of God. He also assisted the other Apostles to be able to do their best to bring glory to the name of the Lord. Let us look at his background and ministry activities in this sermon as follows

DISCUSSION
I.   SILAS HAD HIS NATURAL HUMAN BACKGROUND
    1.   He was a Hellenistic Jew who, it seems, was also a Roman citizen. (Acts 16:37)
    2.   He is also referred to as "Silvanus" in Paul's Epistles. (1 Thessalonians 1:1)
II. SILAS HAD A GOOD MINISTRY BACKROUD
    (1 Peter 5:12) (Acts 15:22) (Acts 15:40-41; 16:25) (Matthew 5:13-14) (Acts 17:14)

CONCLUSION
Many commentators have summed up the life and ministry of Silas in the statement, *"Silas was a faithful and supportive brother who was always bold in adversity."* This is true of Silas in many respects as a faithful worker of Christ as we have seen in his numerous ministry activities in this sermon. The question we

have to ask to end this discussion is this. Can we still get many "Silases" in the Church of Christ today? We are in the end-time period with its numerous challenges. Let us therefore learn precious ministry lessons from Silas.

SIMEON

1
Text: Luke 2:30-32
Theme: Simeon and his Prophecy

INTRODUCTION

Simeon's brief appearance in the New Testament is very important. Although very little is known about him, what he says about the child Jesus, the future saviour and Messiah well ahead of Jesus' earthly ministry is significant. Let us look at some of the facts about this man and his short prophecy in this sermon.

DISCUSSION
I.   SIMEON HAD HIS IDENTITY
     1.   Simeon lived in Jerusalem. (Luke 2:25-26) (Luke 2:29)
II. SIMEON HAD HIS SOURCE OF INSPIRATION
     1. He came under the Spirit's inspiration when the parents brought the child Jesus into the Temple. (Luke 2:26- 27)
III. SIMEON HAD HIS MESSAGE BY PROPHETIC INSIGHT
     (Luke 2:30-32) (Luke 2:33-35)

CONCLUSION

Simeon was a great prophet of God. Through him God could predict that Jesus was going to be the source of the rise and fall for many in Israel. This is what happened in the earthly ministry of Jesus. Those who were genuine in seeking God's salvation got it through Him. Those who were hypocritical and were merely paying lip service to God saw Him as a stumbling block in their way and crucified Him.

STEPHEN

1

Text: Acts 6:5

Theme: The Character profile of Stephen

`

INTRODUCTION

Genuineness of salvation and personal testimony are important pre-requisites to our receiving the fullness of the Holy Spirit. Stephen was an ordinary member of the early church but his conversion and practical life were such that, among the thousands of believers who came into the early church, he was noticed to be chosen as one of the first deacons of the church. His life offers us several challenges as Christians today. Let us look at the details in this sermon.

DISCUSSION

I. STEPHEN HAD HIS INITIAL CALLING (Acts 6:1-7)
    1. Stephen is first mentioned in Acts 6:5 as part of a group of men that were chosen to be deacons.
    2. There arose some problems with Greek widows being neglected in their care. Unfortunately, today most churches continue to neglect widows that are the responsibility of the church. (Acts 6:1) (1 Timothy 5:2-16)
    3. This neglect resulted in the apostles spending precious ministry time to correct this problem. (Acts 6:2)

4. The Apostles dealt with this problem by tasking the local church members to choose deacons who will be entrusted with this work. (Acts 6:3)

5. Stephen became one of these chosen deacons. (Acts 6:5)

2. STEPHEN MET GREAT CONFRONTATION (Acts 6:8 – 7:60) Stephen's new role did not stop with the daily routine of helping elderly widows. He also used his role to do the following:

1. Stephen used part of his time to demonstrate wonders and miracles among the people. (Acts 6:8b)

2. He also contended for the faith. (Acts 6:8a)

3. Depending upon the wisdom of the Holy Spirit, Stephen could refute all the arguments of his opponents. (Acts 6:10)

4. Stephen was consequently brought before the Council and charged with blasphemy. (Acts 6:11-14)

5. Stephen used the opportunity to share the Gospel of Jesus Christ. (Acts 7:1-53)

6. The enemies were enraged and attacked him as a result. (Acts 7:54)

7. Finally, they dragged him outside and stoned him. Stephen thus, became the first martyr of the early church. (Acts 7:57-58)

3. WHAT STEPHEN LEFT BEHIND WAS CONSEQUENTIAL

1. Stephen was a genuine believer living for Christ in truth. (Acts 6:5)

2. Stephen used his position as a deacon to do great things for God. (Acts 6:8)

3. Stephen's arguments showed that he knew God's word very well. (Acts 6:9-10)

4. Stephen's life shows the need to stand upon the truth of God's Word even if this means death. (Acts 6:11-15)
5. Stephen shared the word boldly with his enemies and opponents. (Acts 7:2a)
6. Stephen stood for Christ firmly in his suffering. (Acts 7:54-58)
7. Stephen demonstrated his Spirit-controlled nature even to the point of death. (Acts 7:59-60)

CONCLUSION

Stephen was called into service in the church of Christ. In his faithful service, he was falsely accused and dragged before the Jewish Council. This gave him the opportunity to share the Gospel resulting in his death as the first martyr of the early church. His life lessons as a true servant of the Lord Jesus Christ are also evident in this sermon. May the Holy Spirit fill us like Stephen to be able to perform miracles and wonders for Christ in this evil end-time period.

2

Text: Acts 7:55-56, 60
Theme: Stephen, the man of God

INTRODUCTION

Who is a Man of God? A man of God is that servant who has been called, specially chosen and equipped by God to be used in special ways to bring glory to His name. Stephen was a Man of God because he fits into this definition by his character, conduct and what he allowed God to use him to do in the early church. To understand this title, Man of God, which many people have wrongly been using in the Church today, let us look at some of its characteristics in the life of Stephen from this sermon.

DISCUSSION

I. STEPHEN WAS A MAN OF GODLY CHARACTER
1. He was full of the Holy Spirit. (Acts 6:3, 5) (Luke 12:12) (Galatians 5:22-23)
2. He was full of wisdom. (Acts 6:3, 10; 7:10, 22) (Proverbs 2:6) (Exodus 36:1, 2) (1 Corinthians 1:24)
3. He was full of faith. (Acts 6:5) (Ephesians 1:11, 12)
4. He was full of grace. (Acts 6:8) (John 1:14) (Titus 3:5-6)
5. He was full of power. (Acts 6:8) (1 Corinthians 1:18)
6. Stephen had an angelic countenance though he was an ordinary man. (Acts 6:15)

II. STEPHEN WAS A MAN OF GREAT COURAGE
1. Stephen showed courage in his witness for Christ. (Acts 6:9, 10)
2. Stephen showed courage in opposition to his work for Christ. (Acts 7:1-2a, 51)

3. Stephen's ministry proves that it takes only the Holy Spirit to make converts for Christ. (Acts 7:51, 53) (Galatians 5:16)

CONCLUSION

To explore further who a genuine Man of God is as partly revealed in this discussion about Stephen, let us ask ourselves the following important search questions:

1. How godly should a person be before he can qualify to be called a Man of God?
2. Which of the character qualities Stephen possessed qualified him to be called a Man of God?
3. Which character attitudes of Christ did Stephen demonstrate to establish the truth that he was a genuine Man of God?
4. Can we also be called Men or Women of God after going through this sermon about Stephen?

3

Text: Acts 7:59

Theme: Some important Spiritual Principles and Qualities we can learn from Stephen

INTRODUCTION

Whenever someone genuinely offers himself to God and decides firmly to live for Him and do His work faithfully, the Holy Spirit fills him and equips him for him to be an example to many in the church of Christ. Stephen was one of such people. As such, his life offers us several important spiritual principles and qualities which can be discussed and applied in this sermon as follows:

DISCUSSION
I.   STEPHEN WAS A MAN WHO WAS AVAILABLE TO GOD (Acts 6:15)
II. STEPHEN WAS A MAN WHO WAS FILLED WITH THE SPIRIT OF GOD
     (Acts 6:5)
III. STEPHEN BELIEVED HISTORY WAS UNDER THE CONTROL OF GOD
IV. He believed that God controlled history – past, present and future. (Acts 7:1-53)
V.   STEPHEN HAD GOOD RELATIONSHIPS WITH PEOPLE (Acts 6:1, 2)
VI. STEPHEN WAS A MAN OF GOOD REPUTATION AMONG GOD'S PEOPLE
     (Acts 6:3)
VII. STEPHEN WAS AN EXAMPLE TO GOD'S PEOPLE (Acts 6:8)

CONCLUSION

Stephen was a genuine Man of God with godly principles. It was no wonder the Jews found him so difficult to deal with because of the fullness of the Holy Spirit upon him. He was also unbending in his godly principles and was willing to follow them both in the church and outside. As a result, God was with him everywhere and used him greatly to glorify His name and even to cause the church which was concentrated at Jerusalem to move out and spread into the Roman world through the persecution which followed his martyrdom. God is looking for men like Stephen today who can be available, relatable, exemplary, reputable and full of His spirit to use. Can you or will you be one of such men in the church today wherever you find yourself?

THOMAS

1

Text: John 11:16

Theme: Some admirable traits from Apostle Thomas

INTRODUCTION

Thomas possessed several admirable character qualities. Unfortunately, the only thing people always remember about him is the tag, "the doubting Thomas". But as an Apostle, we should not only look at this faith weakness but go beyond this to see the other good contributions he made to the coming of the New Covenant which constitutes the major reasons why God called him as an apostle. Let us forget about his doubting and look at him from another angle in this sermon and combine it with some other excellent character features to see some of the important truths his normal life can teach us. The details are as follows:

DISCUSSION
I.   THOMAS WAS A MAN OF STRONG PARTNERSHIP
     (John 11:16) (Luke 22:33)
II. THOMAS WAS A MAN OF GREAT PROSPECTS
     (John 14:5)
III. THOMAS WAS A MAN OF PRACTICAL PROOF
     (John 20:24-29) (Mark 16:11-13) (1 Thessalonians 5:21) (John 20:28)

CONCLUSION

Though Thomas was Thomas, we must also understand that in many other ways, he was more than the doubting Thomas as this sermon has shown us. He was a man of great zeal and enthusiasm whose spiritual expectation was also very high. These are positive truths we can learn from him today as Christians who are also patiently waiting for the Lord at the rapture.

2
Text: John 20:27
Theme: The Negative and Positive Characteristics of Apostle Thomas

INTRODUCTION
In normal life situations, we commend or condemn a man by looking at all the facts about him without any bias. This is the only way to make our assessment of him fair and acceptable. This is what we intend to do in this sermon about Apostle Thomas by looking at both the positive and negative character traits he exhibited as an Apostle of the Lord Jesus Christ. An analysis of all the facts about Thomas reveals the following truths about him.

DISCUSSION
I.   THOMAS WAS FULLY DEVOTED TO CHRIST
     (John 11:16; 20:27)
II. THOMAS WAS A CHALLENGING CHARACTER
     (John 20:25)
III. THOMAS WAS ABSENT AT THE APPEARNCE OF CHRIST
     (John 20:24)
IV. THOMAS DOUBTED THE RESURRECTION OF CHRIST
     (Acts 20:25)
V.   THOMAS WAS TOTALLY COMMITTED
     (John 20:26)
VI. THOMAS WAS FINALLY CREDULOUS
     (John 20:28)

CONCLUSION

The sermon we have discussed above reveals the truth about Apostle Thomas that he was a balanced man both spiritually and practically. His demanding practical proof before believing the resurrection of the Lord Jesus Christ did not in any way demean his devotion to Him and to His work.

3

Text: John 11:16

Theme: The background and Life Profile of Apostle Thomas

INTRODUCTION

Thomas was called as one of the Apostles of Jesus Christ who remained loyal to Christ up to the end of his life in ministry. He joined all the other Apostles and disciples in the upper room to wait for the promised out-pouring of the Holy Spirit. Although, we do not hear so much about him after Pentecost, he remained faithful to his calling until he was called home. Some of the facts about his background and life are as follows:

DISCUSSION

I. THE BACKGROUND OF APOSTLE THOMAS
    1. It is generally believed that Thomas was born in the early 1st century CE in Galilee, a region in the Roman province of Judea surrounding the Sea of Galilee.
    2. Thomas had an unnamed twin brother. Thomas means "twin" (from the Greek). Didymus also means "twin" (from Aramaic). (John 11:16, 20:24, 21:2)
    3. He was called as one of the Apostles of Christ. (Matthew 10:2, 3) (Luke 6:15)

II. THE LIFE PROFILE OF APOSTLE THOMAS
    1. He is first mentioned in the Scriptures in Matthew 10:3.
    2. He is finally mentioned in the Scriptures in Acts 1:13.
    3. Tradition says he died in India.
    4. Tradition says he died as a martyr for Christ after being killed by arrows as he was praying.

CONCLUSION

It is important to acknowledge that men like Thomas are always important to God not just because of the major episodes in their lives but also because of their faithfulness and devotion to the Lord Jesus Christ up to the end of their lives. Thomas worked and died as a martyr when he became convinced that Jesus had truly risen from the dead just as he had predicted. How far can we also go with the Lord Jesus Christ today as the time of His appearing draws close?

TIMOTHY

1

Text: 2 Timothy 1:4

Theme: The Birth and Background of Timothy

INTRODUCTION

Timothy was a faithful co-worker of Apostle Paul who became very useful in the ministry of the Lord Jesus Christ. There are a lot of good lessons we can learn from him about involvement in the ministry of the Lord Jesus Christ. But before we do this, let us look at his background and the circumstances of his birth as a preparation for the detailed study of his life and ministry involvement. The simple facts are as follows:

DISCUSSION

I.   TIMOTHY'S NAME MEANS "DEAR TO GOD"

II. TIMOTHY'S MOTHER'S NAME WAS EUNICE WHICH MEANS "GOOD VICTORY" FROM GOD (2 Timothy 1:5)

III. TIMOTHY HAD A GODLY AND DEDICATED GRANDMOTHER

1. She was very instrumental in Timothy's spiritual upbringing. (2 Timothy 1:5) (2 Timothy 3:14, 15)

IV. TIMOTHY'S MOTHER WAS A JEW BUT HIS FATHER WAS A GREEK (Philippians 2:22; Acts 16:1)

V. TIMOTHY WAS PROBABLY BORN AND BRED IN LYSTRA WHICH WAS PROBABLY A CITY IN THE AREA OF GALATIA

1. The exact site of the city of Lystra is uncertain. However, some historians and expositors place it in the region of Galatia Isauria. (Acts 16:1a)

CONCLUSION

Very often in life, what we become as adults and are able to do in life for God depends to a large extent upon where we are coming from and how we were nurtured and brought up. Timothy could become very useful to Apostle Paul and the ministry partly because of the spiritual upbringing he had in a family and home life dominated by sound spiritual and godly principles. So before he grew up, he had a good spiritual foundation already prepared for him by his godly parents. Let Timothy's family life and upbringing be a challenge to us as Christians and Christian parents.

2

Text: Philippians 2:19-24

Theme: The Ministry Involvement of Timothy

INTRODUCTION

Timothy's name means "Dear to God" and truly he lived his life to reflect the meaning of his name. He became dear to God in many ways right from his youthful days. He also became dear to Apostle Paul in his ministry and missionary journeys. His commitments and devotion to the work of Christ was unparalleled. Truly, he was dear to God. Let us seek proof of this in this sermon as follows:

DISCUSSION

I. TIMOTHY WAS TRAINED FOR THE MINISTRY

1. He was initially trained by his mother and his grandmother. (2 Timothy 1:4, 5; 3:14, 15)

2. He was also trained by Apostle Paul. (1 Corinthians 4:17; 1 Timothy 1:2, 18; 2 Timothy 1:2; 3:10, 11)

II. TIMOTHY EXERCISED MULTIPLE MINISTRIES

1. Timothy was an assistant writer to Apostle Paul who assisted in the writing of six of the books of the New Testament. (2 Corinthians 1:1; Philippians 1:1; Colossians 1:1; 1 Thessalonians 1:1; 2 Thessalonians 1:1; Philemon 1:1)

2. He worked as a Missionary. (Acts 16:1, 3, 4)

3. He worked as a divine Messenger. (1 Corinthians 4:17; Philippians 2:19-23; 1 Thessalonians 3:6)

4. He worked as a Teacher. (1 Timothy 4:6, 11, 13, 16)

5. He worked as a faithful Preacher. (2 Timothy 4:2)

6. He worked as an Evangelist. (2 Timothy 4:5)

III. TIMOTHY WORKED WITH APOSTLE PAUL IN MISSIONS

1. As they were going through the cities, they delivered statues from the apostles for them to be observed. (Acts 16:3-4)

2. He went on the second missionary journey with Paul and Silas.

(Philippians 2:19-24) (2 Corinthians 1:19)

3. Timothy was sent to the Philippian church to check on their spiritual condition. (Philippians 2:19, 20)

CONCLUSION

Timothy is an excellent example to all the youth in the church of Christ today as far as faithful and committed ministry in the church of Christ is concerned. A lot of the youth of Christ in the church today are wasting their gifts, talents and abilities on unprofitable things as the souls of men and women pass before them daily into hell. But how did Timothy spend his life as a youth. May the Spirit of the living God rekindle the spirit of Timothy in the hearts of all the numerous young men and women in the Church of Christ today!

3

Text: 1 Timothy 4:12
Theme: Some Practical characteristics of Timothy I

INTRODUCTION

As a young man enlisted in the service of Christ, what were some of the practical characteristics exhibited by Timothy? It is important to learn these important characteristics in this sermon because they pertain to the practical ministry of the church and can be valuable lessons on our involvement in the work of Christ today. Some of these important characteristics can be discussed in this sermon as follows:

DISCUSSION

I.   TIMOTHY HAD A GOOD NAME
     (Acts 16:1, 2)
II. TIMOTHY HAD A GOOD NATURE
     (Philippians 2:22)
III. TIMOTHY WAS SERVICEABLE
     (Acts 18:5; Philippians 2:20-22)
IV. TIMOTHY WAS COMMANDED TO BE STRONG
     (1 Timothy 4:12; 2 Timothy 1:7, 8; 2:1)

CONCLUSION

As discussed in this sermon, Timothy had some characteristics which were very important to successful ministry in God's vineyard. These characteristics are also needed by all faithful workers and servants today. How did young Timothy exercise these ministry characteristics to his success? How can we also succeed today by applying these same principles in the ministry of Christ? We need to follow the example of Timothy in practical terms with the help of the Holy Spirit.

4

Text: 1 Corinthians 4:17
Theme: Some Practical characteristics of Timothy II

INTRODUCTION
The ministry of the Lord Jesus Christ is bringing people to Christ, leading them into salvation, and pastoring them like a good shepherd for them to be able to work out this salvation daily until they finish the Christian journey successfully. As a result, the work of the ministry calls for some personal characteristics which can enhance and promote this work of shepherding. We want to discuss some of these personal characteristics in the life and ministry of Timothy as follows:

DISCUSSION
I. TIMOTHY WAS A MAN OF HUMILITY IN SERVICE
   (Acts 18:5; Philippians 2:22)
II. TIMOTHY WAS AN EXAMPLE OF DEDICATED SERVANTHOOD
   (2 Timothy 4:5; Philippians 2:22)
III. TIMOTHY WAS AN EXAMPLE OF DEDICATED CHRISTIAN SHEPHERDING
   (Romans 16:21; 1 Corinthians 16:10; 1 Thessalonians 3:2; Philemon 1; 2 Timothy 2:15)
IV. TIMOTHY WAS A MAN OF FAITHFULNESS AND STEADFASTNESS
   (1 Corinthians 4:17; Philippians 2:22)

CONCLUSION

Can anyone succeed in the ministry of shepherding without these characteristics discussed in this sermon? Without these characteristics in the life of God's servants, their negative attitudes will scatter and drive away all the sheep instead of bringing them together under one shepherd. If Timothy could serve as a worker in the kingdom of Christ, his positive personal characteristics such as those discussed in this sermon made a great contribution to his successful ministration. What can we again learn from these positive personal attitudes of Timothy in this sermon? We need to be successful. So we must serve faithfully like Timothy!

5

Text: 1 Corinthians 11:1

Theme: Some Practical characteristics of Timothy III

INTRODUCTION

The ministry can never be divested from the personal life of the minister. That was why Apostle Paul said that the believers should imitate him as he also imitates Christ. *"Imitate me, just as I also imitate Christ."* NKJV (1 Corinthians 11:1). This draws our attention to the truth that the personal life of the minister has a direct bearing on his ministry. One good characteristic of Timothy which is worth emulating by all is his desire to live and be an example to all the believers just like Apostle Paul. This was one secret of his success as a worker of Christ. Let us look at some important characteristics of his personal life in relation to his ministry in this sermon. The details include the following:

DISCUSSION

I. TIMOTHY MINISTERED AS A MAN WHO UNDERSTOOD PURITY
   (1 Timothy 4:12)

II. TIMOTHY MINISTERED AS A MAN OF PRIORITIES
    (Philippians 2:19, 20)

III. TIMOTHY MINISTERED AS A TEACHER WHO WAS ALSO A PREACHER
     (1 Corinthians 4:17; 1 Timothy 1:3, 5; 1 Timothy 4:6, 11, 13, 16; 6:17, 18; 2 Timothy 2:2)

IV. TIMOTHY MINISTERED AS A MAN WHO WAS WELL TRAINED AND PREPARED
    (1 Corinthians 4:17; 16:10)

V. TIMOTHY MINISTERED AS A GREAT ENCOURAGER
   AND PROMOTER
   (1 Thessalonians 3:2)

CONCLUSION

If Timothy had not combined a life of purity and genuine concern in his teaching and pastoral ministry, would he have succeeded in what Christ wanted him to do? Absolutely not! His hearers would never have taken him seriously. Similarly, they wouldn't have taken his message. The ministry is not only preaching and teaching but also living out in practical terms what you are preaching and teaching. Timothy must be commended for this attitude which is worth imitating by all workers of Christ today.

6
Text: 2 Timothy 3:10
Theme: Some Practical characteristics of Timothy IV

INTRODUCTION

The ministry into which we have been called is warfare! This explains why the work of the ministry is often explained with the imagery of soldiers engaged in a warfare. This also explains why all ministers and believers are encouraged to put on the whole armour of God daily. With this in view, true ministers of Christ always need character qualities which will help them to be firm and unyielding as true soldiers no matter how fierce the battle becomes. Ministers who lack these character qualities always run away and leave the ministry before they fulfil their call. But Timothy had these essential character qualities also which we can also imitate today. Let us look at some of these positive ministry characteristics in his life as follows:

DISCUSSION
I.   TIMOTHY WAS A MAN OF TRUE PATIENCE
     (2 Timothy 3:10)
II. TIMOTHY WAS A MAN OF CONSTANT PERSEVERANCE
     (2 Tim 3:10, 11)
III. TIMOTHY WAS A MAN OF STRONG FAITH
     (1 Thessalonians 3:2; 2 Timothy 1:5; 1 Timothy 4:12; 2 Timothy 3:10)
IV. TIMOTHY WAS A MAN OF GREAT FIDELITY
     (1 Timothy 6:20, 21)

CONCLUSION

It is always difficult to impart what you do not have in life. This principle also works in the ministry of the Lord Jesus Christ. Before Timothy could encourage others as we have learnt in this sermon, he first had to learn how to encourage himself with good character traits like patience, perseverance and faith in times of difficulties. while all Christians need these character qualities to be able to make it to the gates of heaven, ministers need them more to be able to make it as Christians and true servants of Christ. The time is now. Let us pray and rely upon the Holy Spirit to help us to cultivate these good character traits which are necessary for our success.

7

Text: 2 Timothy 2:15

Theme: Some Practical characteristics of Timothy V

INTRODUCTION

Another important requirement of the ministry of the Lord Jesus Christ is the combination of knowledge with practice. The trend in most churches today is to train their ministers to acquire knowledge and to keep on acquiring it to the neglect of practising it. While knowledge is good for successful ministry, if it is not combined with practice, it becomes useless and dangerous. Apostle Paul did not want Timothy to be like this and encouraged him to combine knowledge with practice. Let us look at the details of this in this sermon.

DISCUSSION

I. APOSTLE PAUL ENCOURAGED TIMOTHY TO STUDY AND KNOW THE SCRIPTURES (2 Timothy 2:15; 3:14, 15)

II. HE ALSO ENCOURAGED HIM TO BE SOUND IN SPEECH (1 Timothy 4:12)

III. HE FURTHER ENCOURAGED HIM TO BE SOUND IN HIS CONDUCT (1 Timothy 4:12; 2 Timothy 3:10)

IV. HE ALSO ENCOURAGED HIM TO BE SINCERE IN PRACTICAL LOVE AND CONCERN (1 Timothy 4:12; 2 Tim 3:10)

CONCLUSION

This sermon is a picture of the perfect combination of knowledge and practise. Timothy was encouraged to learn and continue to learn as he was doing in his family before he came into contact with Apostle Paul. But in addition to this, he was also exhorted to let this knowledge translate into practise for him to be successful in his ministry. Empty knowledge without practise only puffs up but perfect knowledge with practise always leads to progress. So knowledge with practise always is the best ideal to follow after going through this sermon. May we all be guided by God's Holy Spirit to pursue knowledge with practise henceforth.

8

Text: 2 Timothy 2:2

Theme: Some Life truths and lessons we can learn from the Life of Timothy

INTRODUCTION

Life lessons are challenges which are exemplified in a person's life and can be copied, followed and emulated to bring us personal victory and success. The life of Timothy and his association with Apostle Paul presents us with several important life lessons which can be emulated by generations of believers to ensure their personal success and victory. We want to discuss a few of these life lessons in this sermon as follows:

DISCUSSION

I. FAITHFULNESS IN SMALL TASKS LEADS TO GOD'S PROMOTION
(Luke 19:17)

II. THE PREACHING OF GODLINESS DEMANDS THE PRACTISE OF GODLINESS BEFORE GOD'S PEOPLE (Ezra 7:10)

III. WHEN WE START WITH CHRIST, WE MUST ALWAYS PERSEVERE AND FINISH IN GOD'S PRESENCE (Philippians 2:20-22; 2 Timothy 4:16-17)

IV. SOUND CHRISTIAN CHARACTER IN MINISTRY IS AN INDISPENSABLE CHRISTIAN PRACTISE (2 Timothy 3:14; 1 Timothy 4:12-14; John 13:15)

V. WHENEVER AND WHEREVER YOU LOCATE A GENUINE SERVANT OF GOD, MAKE HIM A FATHER AND A PATTERN (2 Timothy 2:2)

CONCLUSION

Christian life lessons can never be learned from people who refuse to obey Christ and do His will. Anytime we hear of positive life lessons, then that person walked well with Christ and his efforts are commendable. If we have these life lessons discussed in this sermon to learn about Timothy, then what are the life lessons we are also going to leave behind for others to emulate after our death? Will your life be worth emulating? If yes, praise be to God. If no, let us understand that it is never too late to start.

9

Text: Acts 16:1-7

Theme: Some good and precious virtues we can learn from Timothy at different stages of his life

INTRODUCTION

Timothy's ministry life moved to different levels at the different stages of his life to correspond to his age. This is important for us to know because effective ministry sometimes also depends upon our physical strength in spite of the fact that spiritually, it is the Holy Spirt who empowers us for ministry. What can we learn from Timothy at the different stages of life in his practical ministry? Some of these virtues can be learnt from his life in this sermon as follows:

DISCUSSION

I. THERE ARE LESSONS WE CAN LEARN FROM TIMOTHY'S EARLY UPBRINGING
   (Acts 16:1; 2 Timothy 1:5) (Acts 16:3-5; 2 Timothy 1:1-5) (2 Timothy 3:14-15)

II. THERE ARE LESSONS WE CAN LEARN FROM TIMOTHY'S DEVOTION TO CHRIST IN PERFECT UNITY
    (Acts 16:1-7) (1 Corinthians 9:19-23)

III. THERE ARE LESSONS WE CAN LEARN FROM TIMOTHY'S TUTELAGE AS AN UNDERSHEPHERD
     (Acts 15:36-41) (1 Timothy 1:18-19) (2 Timothy 4:1-5) (Acts 17:13-15) (1 Corinthians 4:17; 2 Corinthians 1:19) (Philippians 1:1; 2:19) (1 Thessalonians 3:1-10)

IV. THERE ARE LESSONS WE CAN LEARN FROM TIMOTHY
   IN HIS LATTER YEARS AND UNDERTAKINGS
   (1 Timothy 1:18, 19; 2:2)

CONCLUSION

If you follow the life of Timothy, you discover that he was the kind of man that spent his whole life serving in the ministry of the Lord Jesus Christ. In his early years, he lived the hard life that came along with going from town to town with Paul. However, we find that as he aged, he eventually became centrally located and set down roots so that he could invest in the lives of people of all ages. At the same time, Paul used the truth of his final years to teach Timothy an important lesson. That as believers, we need to direct our effort toward serving the Lord no matter where we come from or where we end up.

10

Text: Acts 16:1-2

Theme: Facts and Lessons from Timothy (I)

INTRODUCTION

Depending upon what the preacher wants to impart to his congregation, preaching biographical sermons about Bible characters can be done in bits. This can also be done by the putting together of all the essential facts about the Bible character concerned for this to be presented coherently in one sermon or in one teaching session. For this reason, we want to put together all the essential facts about Timothy in a group of six sermons beginning with this first one to serve this useful purpose for biographical sermon preachers and teachers. A grouping of some of the major facts about Timothy in this first sermon can be done as follows:

DISCUSSION

I. TIMOTHY WAS TAUGHT TO PUT HIS FAITH IN GOD FROM CHILDHOOD
   (Acts 16:1; 2 Timothy 1:5)

II. TIMOTHY GREW UP IN A FAMILY WHICH SHAPED HIS LIFE AND CHARACTER (2 Timothy 3:14, 15)

III. TIMOTHY MAY HAVE HEARD ABOUT CHRIST'S SALVATION DURING PAUL'S FIRST MISSIONARY JOURNEY IN SERVICE (Acts 14:6)

IV. TIMOTHY THEREAFTER COMMITTED HIMSELF TO CHRIST AS HIS SAVIOUR
   (Acts 16:1, 2) (1 Timothy 6:12)

V. APOSTLE PAUL SPENT HIS TIME TO TRAIN TIMOTHY IN SPIRITUAL EXCELLENCE (2 Timothy 3:10)

VI. TIMOTHY HAD SEVERAL IMPRESSIVE CHARACTER ESSENTIALS

1. Paul was impressed by several of these impressive character qualities in Timothy which included his knowledge of Judaism and the Hebrew Scriptures, his Gentile connections through his Greek father, and Timothy's reputation as a devout Christian. (2 Timothy 3:14, 15; Acts 16:1)

CONCLUSION

Exemplary characters in the New Testament deserve special treatment and mention. One of such characters is Timothy whose life has been discussed in these last few pages in this book. In fact, he is a good example in all areas of practical life, spiritual life and ministry life. May we learn precious facts and lessons about him from this sermon and five others which will follow this one in a sequence.

11

Text: I Corinthians 4:15-17

Theme: Facts and Lessons from Timothy (II)

INTRODUCTION

This is the second sermon which groups facts and vital lessons about Timothy to enable us preach biographical sermons and teach biographical lessons on him holistically as intimated in the introduction to the first sermon. The additional facts we have to discuss about him can be done in this sermon as follows:

DISCUSSION

I. APOSTLE PAUL CIRCUMCISED TIMOTHY ON ACCOUNT OF THE JEWS WHO WERE NOT CHRISTIANS (Acts 16:3)

II. IN CONTRAST TO TIMOTHY, PAUL DID NOT CIRCUMCISE TITUS ON ACCOUNT OF THESE SAME JEWS WHO WERE NOT FOR CHRIST (Galatians 2:3)

III. TIMOTHY GREW SPIRITUALLY AFTER HIS CONVERSION (2 Timothy 3:15)

IV. TIMOTHY WORKED WITH APOSTLE PAUL AS A MISSIONARY AND CRUSADER
(Acts 15:19-20; 16:4, 5)

V. TIMOTHY WORKED WITH PAUL AS A TRUSTED COMPANION (2 Timothy 2:2-7)

VI. TIMOTHY BECAME A FAITHFUL MISSIONARY TO THE CHURCH WHICH WAS AT CORINTH (1 Corinthians 4:15-17)

CONCLUSION

The additional facts and lessons presented about Timothy in this sermon are a continuation of the previous ones initiated in the previous sermon to assist biographical sermon preachers and biographical lesson teachers to talk about Timothy in a well-arranged and coherent manner. May this second arrangement also help us as ministers and workers in the church.

12
Text: 1 Timothy 1:18
Theme: Facts and Lessons from Timothy (III)

INTRODUCTION
We want to deal with the third sermon in the series of six sermons which are meant to put facts and lessons on Timothy together in a total and complete manner to support biographical preachers and biographical teachers. This third sermon which deals with many of the details of Timothy as Apostle Paul's son in the ministry have several important lessons for us on practical ministry involvement. These essential details can be discussed in this sermon as follows:

DISCUSSION
I. DURING APOSTLE PAUL'S FIRST ROMAN IMPRISONMENT, TIMOTHY BECAME HIS FAITHFUL MESSENGER (Philippians 2:19; 1:1)
II. TIMOTHY WON GREAT RESPECT BECAUSE HE HAD A HEART FOR MINISTRY
(Philippians 2:20-21)
III. APOSTLE PAUL ALWAYS CONSIDERED TIMOTHY AS HIS SPIRITUAL SON IN MENTORSHIP (2 Timothy 1:2; 2:1) (1 Timothy 1:2)
IV. TIMOTHY OFTEN ACCOMPANIED APOSTLE PAUL ON SOME OF HIS TRAVELS FOR MISSIONS (1 Timothy 1:2, 3)
V. APOSTLE PAUL SENT TIMOTHY TO EPHESUS AS HIS PLACE OF PRACTICAL MINISTRY (1 Timothy 1:3-4)

VI. APOSTLE PAUL GAVE TIMOTHY A LASTING MINISTRY
    TASK AS A FAITHFUL SUPPORTER AND MAINTAINER
    (1 Timothy 1:18, 19)
VII.   TIMOTHY EXCELLED IN HANDLING CONFLICTS IN
    THE CHURCH AS A MEDIATOR (1 Timothy 3:14, 15) (2
    Timothy 3:14; 4:2)

CONCLUSION

This third sermon in this special series can be summed up as
Timothy's practical assistance and support in the ministry of
Apostle Paul, his spiritual father and mentor. It has powerful
lessons on working together in the ministry to bring glory to
Christ and bring us success in the Church of Christ. This is a great
sermon for us all whose facts can be put together to be presented
in a holistic manner by all preachers whenever the occasion calls
for this.

13
Text: 1 Timothy 1:19-20
Theme: Facts and Lessons from Timothy (IV)

INTRODUCTION
This is the fourth in the series of six special sermons on the facts
and lessons from the life and ministry of Timothy. This sermon
focuses on Timothy's spiritual and practical life and their bearing
on his ministry. It contains the following essential facts which are
worth following:

DISCUSSION
I.   TIMOTHY'S SPIRITUAL LIFE AND MINISTRY WAS OF
     GREAT CONCERN TO APOSTLE PAUL (1 Timothy 4:14-15)
II. TIMOTHY EXERCISED GREAT CARE IN HOW HE LIVED
     AND TAUGHT IN THE CHURCH PUBLICLY (1 Timothy
     4:16)
III. TIMOTHY'S LIFE OF ABSTEMIOUSNESS WAS EVIDENT
     IN HIS MINISTRY BOTH PUBLICLY AND PRIVATELY (1
     Timothy 5:22, 23)
IV. TIMOTHY LIVED A LIFE OF COMPLETE YIELDEDNESS
     TO CHRIST TO HELP HIM PROFIT AND PREVAIL
     (1 Timothy 6:11, 12)
V.   TIMOTHY LEARNT HOW TO DEAL WITH THOSE
     DEVIATING FROM THE GOSPEL (1 Timothy 6:20)
VI. TIMOTHY ENJOINED APOSTLE PAUL'S CONTINUOUS
     SUPPORT IN INTERCESSORY PRAYER
     (2 Timothy 1:3, 4)

VII.   APOSTLE PAUL DID HIS BEST TO IMPROVE UPON
       TIMOTHY'S MINISTRY PERFORMANCE AND PROGRESS
       (2 Timothy 1:6, 7)

CONCLUSION

In seeking to present lessons on the spiritual and practical lives
of ministers in a holistic manner, this sermon about Timothy can
be of invaluable help because it contains all the essentials and
facts including even how to handle wayward and backslidden
people in the church. May the facts of this sermon be a reflective
mirror to us as ministers and humble servants of the Lord Jesus
Christ.

14
Text: John 10:11-12
Theme: Facts and Lessons from Timothy (V)

INTRODUCTION
Success in the ministry of the Lord Jesus Christ also depends upon the personal disposition of the worker as regards boldness, fearlessness, confidence and positive faith. Whenever these qualities are combined with love, genuine concern and sympathetic handling of the flock, our success will surely come by the power of the Holy Spirit. The holistic approach to the presentation of these and other allied facts is what this sermon is concerned about. The details are as follows:

DISCUSSION
I. APOSTLE PAUL ENCOURAGED TIMOTHY TO BE FEARLESS AND FULL OF CONFIDENCE. (2 Timothy 1:7)
II. APOSTLE PAUL ENCOURAGED TIMOTHY NOT TO BE ASHAMED OF CHRIST
(2 Timothy 1:8)
III. TIMOTHY WAS ENCOURAGED TO TRUST GOD FOR STRENGTH TO MAINTAIN A LIFE OF RIGTEOUSNESS AND PURITY IN CHARACTER
(2 Timothy 1:9; 2:1)
IV. TIMOTHY WAS ENCOURAGED TO MAINTAIN INTERGRITY IN HIS MINISTRY
(2 Timothy 1:13)
V. TIMOTHY WAS ENCOURAGED TO BE BOLD IN HIS MINISTRATION
(2 Timothy 2:1; 1:7a)

VI. TIMOTHY WAS ENCOURAGED TO PREACH THE GOOD NEWS IN LOVE AND FAITH TO THE BRETHREN (2 Timothy 1:13-14)

VII. TIMOTHY WAS ENCOURAGED TO TRAIN AND RAISE DEPENDABLE BELIEVERS. (2 Timothy 2:2)

CONCLUSION

Good shepherds never abandon the flock in the face of danger because of their boldness and the love and concern they have for the sheep. This was what Christ said in John 10:11-12 in the words: *"I am the good shepherd. The good shepherd gives His life for the sheep. But a hireling, he who is not the shepherd, one who does not own the sheep, sees the wolf coming and leaves the sheep and flees; and the wolf catches the sheep and scatters them."* NKJV. This sermon can be of great help in preaching a holistic sermon on Timothy as a good shepherd in accordance with the facts discussed in this sermon and the facts supplied from Christ in John 10:11-12 above.

15

Text: Hebrew 13:23
Theme: Facts and Lessons from Timothy VI

INTRODUCTION
Ability to defend the truth and remain a faithful servant of Christ throughout our ministry period are some of the greatest challenges in the ministry. Defending the truth is difficult because it always brings criticisms and personal attacks. Remaining a faithful minister of Christ throughout your ministry is also difficult because the devil, his demons and their human collaborators never want this to happen. This last lesson on the facts and lessons from Timothy is however emphatic on this as the only way to please Christ and bring glory to His name. let us look at the details as follows:

DISCUSSION
I.   TIMOTHY WAS ENCOURAGED TO MINISTER TO AVOID ALL TROUBLEMAKERS WITH THEIR USELESS PHILOSOPHIES (2 Timothy 2:14, 15)
II. TIMOTHY WAS ENCOURAGED TO REMAIN FIRM IN THE TRUTHS HE HAD BEEN TAUGHT AND PROFESSED (2 Timothy 3:14)
III. TIMOTHY'S MOTHER AND GRANDMOTHER STARTED HIM WELL WITH THE TRUTH PREACHED (2 Timothy 3:15)
IV. TIMOTHY'S PRIMARY RESPONSIBILITY TOWARDS THE TRUTH WAS TO PREACH AND HAVE IT PROPAGATED (2 Timothy 4:1, 2)

V. TIMOTHY'S MINISTRY ALSO INVOLVED THE STRENGTH TO ENDURE AFFLICTIONS AND PERSECUTIONS (2 Timothy 4:5)

VI. TIMOTHY WAS ENCOURAGED TO UNDERSTAND THAT CHRIST NEEDS FAITHFUL CHRISTIAN SERVICE IN PRACTICE (1 Thessalonians 3:2) (Romans 16:21; 2 Corinthians 1:19) (Acts 20:4)

VII. AS MINISTERS, WE SHOULD ALSO NEVER WAVER AS TRUE DISCIPLES OF CHRIST IN OUR SPIRITUAL PURSUITS (Hebrews 13:23; 12:1-2a)

CONCLUSION

What does Christ expect us to do in the ministry? How does He expect us to do this? With what attitude should we do all the things we are required to do in the ministry? If we want to preach a holistic sermon to answer all these questions, then this is the sermon we must preach using Timothy as a perfect example of these truths. If Timothy fully relying upon the Holy Spirit could do these successfully in his ministry, so can we also do it today by relying upon the same omnipotent Holy Spirit. Amen!

TITUS

1

Text: 2 Corinthians 7:5-7, 13

Theme: What we can learn from Titus today as Christians

INTRODUCTION

Titus also worked to assist Apostle Paul like Timothy. He was very precious and useful to Apostle Paul during their period of association. Because of the sincerity with which he worked with Apostle Paul, his life offers us several good examples on faithful and committed ministry. Let us find out some of the useful things we can learn from him today from this sermon.

DISCUSSION

I. TITUS WAS A MAN WHO WORKED TO BRING HOPE AND COMFORT
   (2 Corinthians 7:5-13; 12:18) (2 Corinthians 1:3-4)

II. TITUS WORKED AS A MAN WHO PROVIDED SUPPORT AND CARE

III. (2 Corinthians 2:13; 8:6) (John 12:26) (Galatians 2:1) (2 Corinthians 8:23; 7:6-7) (Titus 1:4, 5)

IV. TITUS ALWAYS WORKED AS A GOOD LEADER IN THE CONGREGATION
    (Titus 1:5)

V. TITUS WORKED AS A GOOD TEACHER IN THE LORD JESUS CHRIST

(Colossians 3:16) (Titus 2:1)

VI. TITUS LIVED AS A MAN OF WISDOM AND DEEP
SPIRITUAL CONSCIOUSNESS
(Titus 3:1-9; Colossians 1:9) (Job 28:28)

CONCLUSION

Titus is often described by Bible commentators as Titus the dependable character. He is never mentioned as someone involved in any active ministry in the Book of Acts. So what we learn about him comes mainly from the few scattered references about him and the epistle written to him. The lessons outlined about him in this sermon truly qualify him to be called Titus the dependable which is a very good character trait in the ministry worth copying by all today.

2

Text: 2 Corinthians 8:23

Theme: The Life profile and Ministry task of Titus

INTRODUCTION

Titus was in many respects like Timothy as a faithful helper of Apostle Paul. He successfully handled several difficult ministry assignments on behalf of Apostle Paul. Let us look at some of the essential facts of his life and ministry in this sermon as follows:

DISCUSSION

I. TITUS WAS A GENTILE WHO WAS CONVERTED TO CHRIST IN THE MINISTRY OF APOSTLE PAUL (Titus 1:4) (Galatians 2:3)

II. THEREAFTER, HE WAS BROUGHT INTO THE MINISTRY BY CHRIST TO BE A PREACHER (Titus 1:1-4)

III. TITUS BECAME A FAITHFUL SERVANT OF THE LORD JESUS CHRIST, A TRUSTED COMPANION OF APOSTLE PAUL AND AN EARLY CHURCH LEADER (Titus 1:5)

IV. LATER, TITUS WENT TO CORINTH TO SERVE THE CHURCH THERE IN SPIRITUAL LEADERSHIP (2 Corinthians 8:6, 16-17)

V. ON APOSTLE PAUL'S THIRD MISSIONARY JOURNEY, HE ARRIVED IN TROAS AND EXPECTED TO MEET TITUS THERE. NOT FINDING HIM, HE LEFT FOR MACEDONIA (2 Corinthians 2:12-13)

VI. TITUS REJOINED APOSTLE PAUL IN PHILIPPI AND GAVE HIM A GOOD REPORT ON THE CORINTHIAN CHURCH MEMBERSHIP (2 Corinthians 7:6-7, 13-14)

VII. WHEN TITUS RETURNED TO CORINTH, HE DELIVERED THE EPISTLE OF 2 CORINTHIANS AND ORGANIZED A

COLLECTION FOR NEEDY SAINTS IN JERUSALEM (2 Corinthians 8:10, 17, 24)

VIII. SEVERAL YEARS LATER, TITUS AND PAUL TRAVELLED TO THE ISLAND OF CRETE, WHERE TITUS WAS LEFT BEHIND TO CONTINUE AND STRENGTHEN THE WORK THERE WITH THE HELP OF THE LORD JESUS (Titus 1:5a)

IX. TITUS' TASK WAS ADMINISTRATIVE. MOSTLY HE WAS TO MAINTAIN SOUND DOCTRINE AND "STRAIGHTEN OUT WHAT WAS LEFT UNFINISHED AND APPOINT ELDERS IN EVERY TOWN" (Titus 1:5)

X. WHEN ARTEMAS AND TYCHICUS ARRIVED IN CRETE TO DIRECT THE MINISTRY, PAUL SUMMONED TITUS TO JOIN HIM IN NICOPOLIS, A CITY IN THE PROVINCE OF ACHAIA IN WESTERN GREECE TERRITORY (Titus 3:12)

XI. THE LAST MENTION OF TITUS IN THE BIBLE INDICATES THAT HE WAS WITH APOSTLE PAUL DURING HIS FINAL ROMAN IMPRISONMENT (2 Timothy 4:10c)

XII. FROM ROME, TITUS WAS SENT TO EVANGELIZE IN DALMATIA INDEPENDENTLY (2 Timothy 4:10c)

XIII. SCRIPTURE SAYS THAT TITUS HAD A GOD-GIVEN LOVE FOR THE CORINTHIAN BELIEVERS; IN FACT, IN RETURNING TO CORINTH, TITUS WENT "WITH MUCH ENTHUSIASM AND ON HIS OWN INITIATIVE" (2 Corinthians 8:16-17)

CONCLUSION

After going through this sermon, it is evident that Titus was a faithful servant of the Lord Jesus Christ who was also a dedicated supporter of Apostle Paul. Furthermore, it was evident that he was trustworthy and dependable since Apostle Paul appointed him to lead difficult works in Corinth, Crete, and Dalmatia. Truly, he was a good partner and fellow worker as Apostle Paul says. (2 Corinthians 8:23)

> <u>2 Corinthians 8:23</u>
> *"If anyone inquires about Titus, he is my partner and fellow worker concerning you. Or if our brethren are inquired about, they are messengers of the churches, the glory of Christ."* NKJV

NEW TESTAMENT FEMALE CHARACTERS

ANNA, THE PROPHETESS

1
Text: Luke 2:36-38
Theme: Anna, the woman with a Vision and Purpose (I)

INTRODUCTION

We hear of Anna as a prophetess just after Jesus' birth. Her name which is of Hebrew origin means "Gracious" or "Merciful". She received God's mercy and grace to witness the birth of the Lord Jesus Christ at the time she was well advanced in age. What lessons can we learn from her in this sermon? Let us discuss the details as follows:

DISCUSSION
I.   SHE WAS COMMITTED (Romans 5:3-5) (Luke 2:37b)
II. SHE HAD A LOT OF COURAGE (1 Corinthians 16:13) (Luke 2:38)
III. SHE WAS STRONG IN FAITH (Hebrews 12:1-3) (Luke 2:37c)
IV. SHE WAS FAITHFUL (1 Peter 4:10-11) (Luke 2:36-37a)
V.   SHE WAS STRONG AND FORCEFUL (Psalm 138:7-8) (Luke 2:38)

CONCLUSION

Few people at the age of Anna will be fasting and praying in the Temple both day and night in the expectation of the Messiah. But Anna did her best to remain faithful to God in spite of her age. We also need her qualities outlined in this sermon to be able to excel for God against all impediments and obstacles until He calls us home.

2

Text: Luke 2:36-38

Theme: Anna, the woman with a Vision and Purpose (II)

INTRODUCTION

Anna was truly a committed and devoted old lady. Her husband died only seven years after they had married. The natural option for Anna would have been getting married to another man, having children and doing what was normal for all women at that time but she chose to remain single and always be in the presence of the Lord in the temple until she was 84 years by the time Christ was born. She was a unique woman of faith. Her life offers us several challenges as Christians today. What are some of them? Let us try to discuss them in this sermon:

DISCUSSION

I.   ANNA RELIED ON GOD'S PROVIDENCE (Psalm 17:5-6) (Luke 2:37c)

II. THROUGH HER FASTING, ANNA SAW GOD'S POWER (Acts 14:22) (Luke 2:37c)

III. ANNA LISTENED TO GOD FOR DIRECTION AND PROGRESS (2 Corinthians 5:16-17) (Luke 2:38)

IV. ANNA UNDERSTOOD WHAT WAS PATIENCE (Colossians 1:11) (Luke 2:37b)

V.   ANNA WORKED FOR CHRIST IN STRONG PARTNERSHIP (1 John 2:28) (Luke 2:38)

CONCLUSION

The meaning of Anna's name (Gracious or Merciful) and the meaning of the tribe she comes from ("Blessed") combined to make her favoured, unique and blessed among women. Few women can do what she did up till her age until they are rewarded by God with great events such as her seeing the birth of the Messiah and the Saviour of the whole world.

DORCAS

Text: Acts 9:36-42
Theme: The story of Dorcas' life (Her early life)

INTRODUCTION

Dorcas, or Tabitha, lived in Joppa. Joppa was an important seaport on the Mediterranean coast. She worked as a seamstress in this city and gave her life to Christ. She personally became committed to activities that brough great relief to the needy, especially widows in and around Joppa. This brought her great fame and favour from everybody especially the Christians who saw her as a big asset to the church. The story of her early life in the Bible contains the following details:

DISCUSSION

I.   DORCAS LIVED AS A DISCIPLE OF CHRIST (Acts 9:36a)

II. GENERALLY, DORCAS WAS A WOMAN WHO WAS GOOD AND COMPASSIONATE (Acts 9:36b)

III. PRACTICALLY, DORCAS WAS A WOMAN OF FULL OF GOOD WORKS (Acts 9:36b)

IV. DORCAS LIVED AS A WOMAN WHO ESCHEWED EVIL AND SHUNNED WICKEDNESS (Acts 9:36b)

V.   DORCAS WAS ALSO A PERSON WHO WAS COMMITTED TO CHARITABLE ACTS (Acts 9:39b)

VI. CONSEQUENTLY, DORCAS WAS LOVED BY ALL THE SAINTS FOR HER ACTIONS (Acts 9:40a)

VII.	DORCAS LIVED AS AN ALMS GIVER IN THE CHURCH (Acts 9:36b)

VIII.	DORCAS' LIFE PORTRAYED HER AS A GIVER WHO WAS CHEERFUL (Acts 9:39b)

IX. DORCAS' GIVING WAS OFTEN FOCUSED ON WIDOWS (Acts 9:41)

X.	THIS MEANS SHE HAD PITY FOR WIDOWS AND ALWAYS MOVED TO CARE FOR THEIR WELFARE (Acts 9:39b)

XI. ONE CHARITABLE ACT ON HER PART WAS GIVING CLOTHES TO THE NEEDY (Acts 9:39b)

XII.	MANY OF THE CHRISTIANS SPOKE WELL OF HER BECAUSE SHE HAD A GOOD NAME (Acts 9:36, 39)

CONCLUSION

Dorcas' early life was full of grace, compassion and care for others. Many people are selfish and possessive. Dorcas was the opposite of this negative attitude. This is the reason why her early life was seen as offering some of the greatest challenges on charity. What are some of the personal lessons you have drawn after going through this sermon.

2

Text: Acts 9:36-42

Theme: The story of Dorcas' life (Her latter life)

INTRODUCTION

Though Dorcas was a good woman, one day she fell sick and passed away. Everyone felt sorry for this because of her good deeds and charitable acts. This is evidenced by the many who gathered to mourn her. This also explains why all the believers rushed to seek help from Apostle Peter for prayer for her. Apostle Peter may have partly responded to the pleas of the people after he had heard of her sacrificial service to the Lord in that area. Let us look at this and other details in the story of the latter part of Dorcas' life. The details go this way:

DISCUSSION

I. FOR SOME UNKNOWN REASON, DORCAS DIED SUDDENLY (Acts 9:37)

II. WHEN SHE DIED, THE BELIEVERS REFUSED TO BURY HER BUT RATHER CALLED FOR APOSTLE PETER TO COME AND RENDER SPIRITUAL SUPPORT

1. The purpose was to pray for her resurrection from dead because she was extremely valuable. (Acts 9:40)

III. APOSTLE PETER CAME AND PRAYED FOR HER SUSTENANCE

1. This brought her back to life in great surprise. (Acts 9:40, 41)

IV. HER GOOD WORKS REVERSED HER PREMATURE DEATH

1. All the people around her loved her good works and wanted her to live long. (Acts 9:39)

V. EVEN HEAVEN LOVED HER GOOD WORKS AND SENT HER BACK INTO THE WORLD TO CONTINUE HER CHARITABLE DEEDS (Acts 9:41-42a)

VI. UNTIL GOD FINISHES WHAT HE WANTS TO USE YOU TO DO FOR PEOPLE AND IN HIS CHURCH, NOBODY CAN TAKE YOU OUT OF YOUR DEDICATION (Acts 9:38)

VII. DORCAS' MIRACLE BROUGHT MANY TO CHRIST AFTER HER RESURRECTION FROM DEATH (Acts 9:42)

CONCLUSION

Whatever we do on earth for people, Heaven watches us. God who has filled every part of creation with His Spirit is everywhere at the same time. This means no good work goes on without His notice because He is a rewarder of those who diligently seek and do His work faithfully. He rewards all forms of good works from heaven. He did it for Dorcas. He still does it today. But do you qualify to receive the grace Dorcas received by your faithfulness to God and good works in the Church today?

3

Text: Acts 9:36b

Theme: Precious Lessons from the Life of Dorcas

INTRODUCTION

The story of Dorcas has been an inspiration to thousands of ordinary people and thousands of Christians. It is full of valuable lessons, all of which are important, and some of which need particular emphasis in this end-time period in the church of the Lord Jesus Christ. We know very little about the personal background of Dorcas, her age, her status in life – whether she was a married person, or whether she was very rich or poor. But we do know that she "was always doing good and helping the poor". Her name means 'gazelle" or "antelope", or "full of grace." What are some of the precious lessons we can also learn from Dorcas in this sermon? Let us try to discuss the following:

DISCUSSION

I.   DORCAS' LIFE CALLS FOR ATTENTION
   1. She was very industrious. (Acts 9:39b)
   2. She was very compassionate. (Acts 9:39b)
   3. She was very charitable. (Acts 9:36b, 39b)
   4. She was totally selfless. (Acts 9:36b)
   5. She was full of Grace. (Acts 9:36, 39)

II. DORCAS' LIFE WAS TRULY ALTRUISTIC
   1. She used her gifts in service to other people. (Acts 9:39b)
   2. She was committed in doing good for others. (2 Thessalonians 3:13) (Acts 9:36b)
   3. She built supportive relationships with other people. (Acts 9:41)

4. Her ministry to others was unique. (Ephesians 2:10) (Acts 9:36b, 39b)
5. She was a challenge to all sincere Christians. (Acts 9:42)

CONCLUSION

A close study of Dorcas' life makes us aware that it is not surprising that she is a challenge to many people in life and in the church. Her concern for others, widows and other deprived persons, her commitment to using her own resources for the betterment of others and her unselfishness offer precious lessons to the world and to all sincere Christians. Her life will forever remain a challenge!

MARY MAGDALENE

1

Text: Luke 8:2

Theme: Precious Lessons from the Life of Mary Magdalene I

INTRODUCTION

Mary Magdalene is one woman in the New Testament whose life and devotion to Jesus offer several precious lessons to believers. We want to look at some of these lessons in this sermon and see how they can help us in our walk with the Lord Jesus.

DISCUSSION

I.   MARY MAGDALENE WAS THE FIRST WOMAN TO HEAR ABOUT THE RESURRECTION OF THE LORD JESUS CHRIST (Matthew 28:1, 5-7)

II. MARY MAGDALENE IS A PICTURE OF THE DELIVERANCE POWER OF THE LORD JESUS CHRIST (Luke 8:2; Matthew 28:18)

III. MARY MAGDALENE IS AN EXAMPLE OF WALKING WITH JESUS WITH PERSISTENCE (Mark 15:40)

IV. MARY MAGDALENE WAS A WOMAN OF FAITH, HOPE AND PERSUASION (Luke 24:6-8)

CONCLUSION

As we have seen in this sermon, though Mary Magdalene came to Jesus with a great spiritual disadvantage, when she got the opportunity to serve Christ, she did it with her whole heart and followed Him to the time of His death and resurrection. It was no wonder she continued with the disciples after the ascension of Christ. This partly explains why some people call her "the woman Apostle of the Lord Jesus Christ."

2

Text: Luke 8:2

Theme: Precious Lessons from the Life of Mary Magdalene II

INTRODUCTION

As already mentioned in part 1 of this sermon, the life of Mary Magdalene offers believers several precious lessons and challenges today. In this second sermon, we want to look at more of these challenges and how they can help us to walk aright with God today.

DISCUSSION

I. MARY MAGDALENE WAS A WOMAN FULL OF GRATITUDE
   (Luke 8:2; 1 Thessalonians 5:18)

II. MARY MAGDALENE IS AN EXAMPLE THAT JESUS KNOWS US ALL BY NAME AND GENDER
   (Isaiah 43:1; Daniel 2:22; Luke 12:2-3)

III. MARY'S LIFE IS A FULFILMENT OF SEEKING GOD GENUINELY
   (Mathew 6:33; Colossians 2:6-7)

IV. MARY MAGDALENE IS AN EXAMPLE OF WHAT WOMEN CAN ALSO DO TO HELP SPREAD THE GOOD NEWS OF THE GOSPEL
   (Matthew 28:18-20, Acts 1:8, 14)

CONCLUSION

What additional lessons can we learn of Mary Magdalene in this sermon? There are several lessons we can draw from her life here but there is one I want to emphasize here. This is the task of sharing the Good News of Salvation with the lost world. Is this the reserve of men or the whole church including the women? Mary's life shows that women can also be effective tools in evangelism and the propagation of the Gospel.

3

Text: John 20:1

Theme: Five Notable things to note about Mary Magdalene

INTRODUCTION

Jesus' preaching, teaching and healing ministry always went with a powerful deliverance ministry. People held in bondage to sin and Satan always got their freedom anytime they came to Him. Mary Magdalene was one of such fortunate seekers who became totally liberated through the deliverance accorded her by the Lord Jesus Christ. She thereafter became very useful to Christ and His ministry. Some of the notable facts about her include the following:

DISCUSSION

I. WHY WAS MARY CALLED MAGDALENE?
    1. She was from Magdala, a thriving fishing town on the coast of Galilee which was famous for producing prostitutes. (Luke 8:1-2)
    2. But Mary became a repentant prostitute upon meeting Jesus. (John 19:25)

II. WHAT DID MARY DO TO HELP JESUS' MINISTRY?
    1. She always travelled with Jesus and His disciples. (Luke 8:2-3) (John 20:1) (Matthew 27:55-56a)
    2. She did her best to provide funds for Jesus' ministry. (Luke 8:1-3)

III. WHY WAS MARY GIVEN A NAME WITH MEANING?
    1. Consequently, she is always referred to as the "Apostle to the Apostles" because she was the first person to see the risen

Christ and the first to share the news of the resurrection with the disciples. (Matthew 28:1, 5-8)

CONCLUSION

There was no woman among the Apostles of Christ. But many expositors believe that if Christ had included women among his disciples, Mary Magdalene would have been her first choice. She went everywhere with them throughout Christ's earthly ministry until all of them ended up in the upper room to wait for the Pentecost. So in a sense, she was an apostle in disguise. Though she worked at the background, she was extremely useful to the ministry of Christ and the apostles.

MARY, MOTHER OF JESUS

1

Text: Luke 1:26-27
Theme: Mary and the visit of Angel Gabriel

INTRODUCTION

It is a true statement that God moves in mysterious ways to perform His wonders. He moved in this special way in the life of the young virgin Mary to perform a great wonder which did not have any precedent in the life of man since creation. The wonder was the promise of the conception of Jesus. But this came to pass exactly as the Angel Gabriel was sent to inform Mary. Let us look at the details of this visit by Angel Gabriel in this sermon.

DISCUSSION
I. MARY WAS VISITED BY THE ANGEL GABRIEL
    (Luke 1:26-27)
II. GABRIEL BROUGHT MARY A MESSAGE WHICH WAS GOOD
    (Luke 1:28)
III. GABRIEL BROUGHT A UNIVERSAL MESSAGE WHICH WAS GREAT
    (Luke 1:30-35)

"

CONCLUSION

This promise of the miraculous conception of the Lord Jesus did not have a precedent. Ever since it took place, it has also not had anything comparable to it in the whole of creation. And surely it is not going to have any equal until the end of the world. This is one truth which makes Jesus unique and the messiah worth following for our eternal salvation. But the challenge comes in here. Why did God choose the virgin Mary for this great miracle among all the young women in Israel at that time? The first reason was probably because of God's sovereign election. But the second reason could be the unique characteristics and capabilities Mary possessed as a young lady. What can we also do today in the Church of the Lord Jesus Christ to make it possible for God to use us as He used the virgin Mary?

2

Text: Ephesians 1:4

Theme: Some Prominent features in the life of Mary, the mother of Jesus

INTROUDCTION

Whenever and wherever the name of Mary, the mother of Jesus is mentioned, it brings great glorification to womanhood. It glorifies women as extremely important in the economy of God who are also important in the fulfilment of all the plans of God on earth. Even the saviour of the whole universe could not come into the world without God using a woman. If this was the case, then in what other way can we dispense with women in the world? Let us look at some of the important features of this great woman who availed herself to God in this sermon. They are as follows:

DISCUSSION

I.   SHE WAS A WOMAN WHOSE LIFE WAS PREDICTED AND CONFIRMED (Isaiah 7:14; Matthew 1:23)

II. SHE WAS A WOMAN OF FAITH AND COURAGE

   1. She exhibited great faith and courage in accepting what was humanly impossible. (Luke 1:38)

   2. By her faith and courage, she believed Jesus could miraculously provide wine at the wedding at Cana. (John 2:3)

   3. She believed she could find Jesus when He was left in the temple. (Luke 2:48)

III. MARY WAS A WOMAN WHO WAS GREAT AND SPIRITUALLY CAUTIOUS

   1. Her words in the Magnificat portray her as such. (Luke 1:46-49)

IV. MARY WAS A WOMAN WHO WAS TRULY CONCERNED
    1. She was present at the crucifixion. (John 19:25)
    2. She was present at the upper room. (Acts 1:14)
V.   MARY WAS A WOMAN WHO UNDERSTOOD TRUE HOLINESS AND CONSECRATION
    1. She maintained her virginity to be able to give birth to Christ. (Isaiah 7:14; Matthew 1:23) (Matthew 1:25)

CONCLUSION

If the Lord God chose Mary and used her as the mother of the great redeemer Jesus, He had very good reasons for doing this. As we have seen in this sermon, Mary possessed all the necessary spiritual and practical features needed for the fulfilment of this great plan of God, and naturally when God looked round He picked her. The challenge then comes to all young men and women in the Church of Christ: "can the Lord God find all these good features of Mary in me today if He wants to reenact the story of the birth of the Lord Jesus?"

3

Text: Hebrews 2:12 with Luke 1:46-49
Theme: Mary and the importance of Praise

INTRODUCTION

Praise naturally flows from us in times of joy, good news and acceptance but it is not normal for praise to flow from our lips in times of shame, ridicule and social defamation. Mary is one person who had nothing socially to praise God for, for her conception of Jesus because it exposed her to social shame as a woman who has become unfaithful to her husband and had gone to flirt with other men to become pregnant at her betrothal stage. That she could set aside all these and praise God in her condition is a virtue worth discussing in this sermon. This praise which has become known as the Magnificat can be analysed as follows:

DISCUSSION

I. THIS PRAISE TOOK PLACE DURING HER VISIT TO ELIZABETH (Luke 1:39-40)

II. THIS PRAISE TOOK PLACE OUT OF GREAT ELATION (Luke 1:46, 47)

III. THIS PRAISE BROUGHT MARY GREAT ENCOURAGEMENT (Luke 1:48-49)

CONCLUSION

It is often said that there is power in praises because the Bible clearly states that God dwells in the midst of the praises of His people. "Yet you are holy, enthroned on the praises of Israel." (Psalm 22:3). The Bible has several records of people seeing the great hand of God when they praised Him in their difficulties. Mary's praise in adverse circumstances also brought her great victory and enabled God to use her in one of His greatest plans for mankind on earth.

MARY OF BETHANY

1

Text: John 11:2

Theme: Mary of Bethany, the woman who wanted to become the true disciple of Christ

INTRODUCTION

Jesus taught during His earthly ministry that one of the requirements of true discipleship is the willingness to forsake all for His sake. The life of Mary of Bethany is an epitome of this teaching because of the way she sacrificed her costly perfume to anoint the body of Jesus just before his death. Let us examine this truth in this sermon as follows:

DISCUSSION
I. MARY WAS A DISCIPLE WHO WANTED TO WALK IN THE STEPS OF JESUS (Luke 9:23-24; John 12:1-8; Mark 14:1-8)
II. MARY WAS A DISCIPLE WHO BORE TESTIMONY TO GLORIFY JESUS (Matthew 26:6-13) (Matthew 26:13; Mark 14:9)

CONCLUSION

In one of His teachings Jesus made it clear to the religious leaders of His day that ordinary people will come from far and wide, from remote areas, and from inaccessible areas to seek His salvation and obtain it while the so-called teachers of the law and the prejudiced Jews continue to grope in the darkness out of ignorance. This came to pass even before Jesus died and went back to the Father in the lives of devoted but unrecognized women like Mary of Bethany who could recognize Jesus as the Messiah and glorify Him before He died. People like Mary will be seen in the kingdom of the Father. But how many of the antagonistic pharisees and religious leaders will be there? Let us learn to walk in the steps of people like Mary of Bethany.

2

Text: John 11:40

Theme: Some Noble characteristics of Christian Womanhood

INTRODUCTION

Women played very important roles in the earthly ministry of the Lord Jesus Christ. It was a woman who gave birth to Christ Himself. It was women like Mary Magdalene, Joana and the rest who saw to the physical needs of Christ and His disciples. It was a woman like Mary Magdalene who was the first to see Christ after His resurrection. Christian womanhood showed up prominently in the ministry of Christ. Let us learn some precious lessons on Christian womanhood in this sermon. It shows in the following ways:

DISCUSSION

I.   IT SHOWS IN TOTAL DEVOTION TO GOD (Luke 10:38-42)

II. IT SHOWS IN TOTAL FAITH IN GOD
     (John 11:32-36; 38-44)

III. IT SHOWS IN SINCERE SACRIFICE TO GOD (Matthew 26:6-13; Mark 14:3-9; John 12:1-3)

CONCLUSION

If women were used to glorify God as we have seen in this sermon, what can women in the Church of the Lord Jesus Christ today also do with their lives to bring glory to God? At least this sermon has taught us that women can be examples of total devotion to God, examples of faith in difficult situations, and examples of precious sacrifice to bring glory to God. What can you also do as a woman?

3

Text: Matthew 26:6-13
Theme: The Alabaster jar of Mary of Bethany

INTRODUCTION
The Alabaster jar of perfume of Mary of Bethany has become a symbol of sacrifice, selflessness, devotion, and dedication. Truly Mary did very well in her action which deserves constant commendation. We want to look at the details of this singular action which dominates all the good things Mary did as a character in the New Testament. It is worth remembering that this action bears the following indelible features:

DISCUSSION
I. THE ACTION WAS COSTLY
    (John 12:3-5; Matthew 20:2)
II. THE ACTION WAS CRITICIZED
    (John 12:4-6)
III. BUT THE ACTION BECAME COMMEMORATIVE
    (Matthew 26:13; Mark 14:9)

CONCLUSION
To be commended by Jesus and approved for everlasting remembrance by no less a person than the Lord Jesus Christ Himself is a great feat. Mary of Bethany did what she did for Jesus out of the bottom of her heart. Jesus who was divine saw this and gave her the best commendation possible. What can we also do in the Church of the Lord Jesus Christ today to merit His commendation? Let this great challenge come to us personally and individually.

4

Text: John 11:32-33
Theme: Some salient facts in the life of Mary of Bethany

INTRODUCTION

Mary of Bethany is a woman whose life is full of great and interesting episodes. Because these episodes offer us great spiritual and practical lessons, we want to examine some of the prominent ones in this sermon as follows:

DISCUSSION
I.   HER NAME IS A BLESSING
    1. It means "star of the sea" or "beloved."
II. MARY WAS A NATIVE OF BETHANY
    1. Her sister was Martha and her brother was Lazarus. (John 11:1-2)
III. MARY DEFIED CULTURAL PREJUDICE AND SAT AT THE FEET OF JESUS HER BENEFACTOR
    1. She defied cultural prejudice and sat together with the men at the feet of Jesus. (Luke 10:39)
IV. MARY ANOINTED JESUS TO PREPARE HIM FOR BURIAL
    1. Mary anointed Jesus with an alabaster jar of very expensive oil. (Matthew 26:7; Mark 14:3b; John 12:3)
V.   JESUS DEFENDED MARY'S BENEVOLENCE
    1. Jesus defended Mary's actions against all criticisms. (Matthew 26:10; Mark 14:6; John 12:7)
VI. MARY'S ACTIONS BROUGHT HER EVERLATING BLESSINGS

1. Christ said her actions will be remembered forever. (Matthew 26:13; Mark 14:9)

VII.   MARY ALWAYS CHOSE THAT WHICH WAS THE BEST

1. She chose to listen to Jesus than to prepare and serve meals. (Luke 10: 40-42)

VIII.   MARY SHOWED GREAT PRACTICAL LOVE FOR HER BROTHER

1. She and her sister Martha informed Jesus that their brother Lazarus was sick. (John 11:3)

IX. SHE WAITED EXPECTANTLY FOR JESUS' REACTION AND QUICK BUSINESS

1. She waited expectantly for Jesus' arrival to attend to her brother. (John 11:28-33)

X. MARY WEPT THINKING SHE WAS BEREAVED

1. She wept at the death of her brother Lazarus. (John 11:32-33)

CONCLUSION

Looking at these events listed and discussed above about Mary of Bethany in this sermon, what are some of the spiritual and practical lessons we can draw from them? They are many but some of the interesting ones are her devotion to Jesus, love for her brother Lazarus, belief in the power of prayer for her brother Lazarus' healing, concern for spiritual things over and above the material, and several others.

MARTHA

1

Text: Psalm 37:1

Theme: Some important facts about Martha, the Sister of Mary of Bethany

INTRODUCTION

The most important thing most people know about Martha in the New Testament was her getting preoccupied to serve Jesus and attend to his material needs instead of sitting at His feet to receive teaching as her sister Mary did. But apart from this, there are some good things we can learn from the life of Martha. Even there was nothing wrong with this act of seeking to serve Jesus except that its timing was wrong and it was given unnecessary pre-eminence over that which was spiritual which was the first thing she should have sought from a busy person like Jesus who was not easy to get in a private home as she got with her sister Mary. What are some of the other useful facts we can learn from Martha? Let us look at some of them in this sermon as follows:

DISCUSSION

I. MARTHA HAD A NAME WHICH MADE HER A MISTRESS

1. The name Martha means, "Lady Boss", "Land Lady" or "Mistress."

II. MARTHA WAS THE SISTER OF LAZARUS AND MARY

1. Martha, Mary and Lazarus were family relatives. (John 11:1, 2)

III. MARTHA WAS A WOMAN WHO WAS HUMBLE

1. She did not rebuke her sister Mary openly but instead spoke to Jesus to talk to her. (Luke 10:40b) (Colossians 3:23)

IV. MARTHA WORKED AS A WOMAN WHO CARED FOR THE HOME

1. He did what was humanly possible to provide for Jesus and the home. (Luke 10:40a)

V. MARTHA WAS A WOMAN WHO WAS GENTLE AND HUMANE

1. When Jesus spoke to her about her sister she calmed down and did what she was told to do. (Luke 10:41, 42)

VI. MARTHA WAS TAUGHT THE IMPORTANCE OF SPIRITUAL FELLOWSHIP

1. Jesus taught Martha the importance of giving fellowship with God a priority. (Luke 10:39, 42) (Matthew 11:28; Matthew 6:33)

VII. MARTHA WAS TAUGHT THE IMPORTANCE OF REMAINING BOTH SPIRITUALLY BALANCED AND FOCUSED

1. Martha was shown the importance of maintaining a double focus as sane children of God. (Luke 10:42a) (1 Thessalonians 4:11; Luke 13:24)

VIII. MARTHA TEACHES US THE IMPORTANCE OF CARRYING EVERYTHING TO THE LORD

1. When she had a problem with Mary, she went to the Lord. When her brother Lazarus died, she went to the Lord. (Luke 10:40) (1 Peter 5:7; 2 Corinthian 1:3-4) (John 11:3)

IX. MARTHA SHOWS US THE IMPORTANCE OF BROTHERLY LOVE
1. Martha showed deep love for her brother Lazarus and we should also show love for all the brethren. (Romans 12:9-10) (John 11:21)

X. MARTHA'S LIFE SHOWS US THE USELESSNESS OF WORRYING ABOUT LANGUOR
1. Martha worried about her sister Mary which was unnecessary at the time Christ visited them. (Psalm 37:1) (Luke 10:41-42a)

CONCLUSION

Though the Bible says that we should be our brother's keeper and carry one another's burden, it does not teach us to be overburdened to the point of being crushed under the load of worries, unnecessary fears, and unnecessary expectations. Rather in the midst of all these, we should do our best to remain balanced both spiritually and physically so that we can continue to press on in the Lord without any unnecessary distractions. Let the life of Martha emphasize these truths in our lives.

LYDIA

1

Text: Acts 16:13-14a
Theme: Lydia, the noble woman of God

INTRODUCTION
Lydia had a beautiful name which reflected in her life. In God's economy, she became one of the noble women in the early church. Though she is briefly mentioned in the scriptures in Acts 16, her role as a Christian gives us several important practical and spiritual lessons as follows:

DISCUSSION

I.   LYDIA HAD A GOOD NAME AND GREAT PROMINENCE
    1. Lydia was a woman who became prominent at the Church at Philippi. (Acts 16:14a)
    2. Her name Lydia means "beautiful one" or "noble one."

II. LYDIA HAD A GOOD BUSINESS AND GREAT POSSESSIONS
    1. She was a seller of purple. (Acts 16:14b)
    2. This business brought her great wealth. (Acts 16:14) (1 Samuel 2:7-9)

III. LYDIA HAD GREAT COURAGE IN PROTECTION
    1. She hosted apostle Paul and his team in her house. (Acts 16:15b)

2. She defied all the odds and Jewish prejudice to house a Christian church in her home. (Acts 16:40)

IV. LYDIA HAD GREAT FAITH AND MINISTRY PARTNERSHIP
1. Lydia probably started as a convert to Judaism. (Acts 16:15)
2. She later became converted and received Christ through Paul's ministry. (Acts 16:14)
3. She then became a partner in the spread of the gospel. (Luke 10:5-7) (Acts 16:40)

V. LYDIA WAS THE SAMARITAN WOMAN'S PARALLEL
1. Jesus met the Samaritan woman on Jacob's well at Sychar. (John 4:5-7)
2. Paul also met Lydia on the riverside. (Acts 16:13-14a)

CONCLUSION

There are some people who are born to burn for Christ in His work and ministry. Lydia is an example of such people. After embracing Christ, she was bold to house God's people in her home and open her home fully to the preaching and teaching of the gospel. She also supported God's workers materially. These are good examples worth emulating by all the genuine children of God.

2

Text: Philippians 4:8
Theme: Some spiritual lessons from the life of Lydia

INTRODUCTION
Though Lydia is briefly mentioned in the New Testament, our study
of her life will not be complete without a mention of some of the
spiritual lessons her life offers us today as Christians. We want to
look at some of them in this sermon as follows:

DISCUSSION
I. SHE WAS A WOMAN WHO LOVED PRAYER
   (Acts 16:13-14a)
II. SHE WAS A WOMAN WHO LOVED WORSHIP AND
    PRAISES
    (Acts 16:14b) (John 4:24)
III. SHE WAS A WOMAN WHO WAS HOSPITABLE
     (Acts 16:15) (Hebrews 13:2)
IV. SHE WAS A WOMAN WHO BROUGHT COMFORT AND
    HOPE
    (Acts 16:40) (1 Thessalonians 5:11)

CONCLUSION
As the text chosen for this sermon says, our meditation must always
focus on that which is true, noble, just, pure, lovely, of good report
and praiseworthy. These are some of the truths exemplified by
Lydia in this sermon for our emulation as serious and committed
Christians. May we strive and contend for the gospel as she did!

JOANNA

1

Text: Luke 8:19-21

Theme: Joanna, the woman who followed and cared for Jesus and His disciples

INTRODUCTION

Publicly many people know that Jesus always moved with His twelve disciples into towns, villages and cities to preach. But many people do not know that several devoted women followed them privately and unknowingly. One of such women was Mary Magdalene. Another was Joanna whose name means "God is gracious." Truly, she lived as a woman full of grace as she accompanied Jesus and His disciples on their itinerant preaching. What lessons can we learn from Joanna in this sermon? There are several including the following:

DISCUSSION

I. JOANNA HAD A GOOD AND RESPECTABLE SOCIAL BACKGROUND

1. Joanna was the wife of Chuza, Herod's steward who was in charge of his domestic affairs. (Luke 8:3a)
2. Joanna was one of several afflicted women like Mary Magdalene who were delivered by Jesus (Luke 8:2-3a)

II. JOANNA HAD A SPIRIT OF BENEVOLENCE

1. Together with the other delivered and devoted women, Joanna always travelled with Jesus and His disciples to see to their physical and material needs. (Luke 8:3b)
2. Because Jesus and His disciples could not do any secular work during the earthly ministry of Jesus, women like Joanna and her friends used their money, goods and properties to provide for their needs. (Luke 8:3b) (Mark 15:41)

III. AFTER CHRIST'S DEATH JOANNA STILL SHOWED GOOD BEHAVIOUR
1. Joanna continued to follow and serve Jesus up to the time of His death. (Mark 15:39-41)
2. Though it is not specifically mentioned, it is possible that because of her devotion to Jesus, Joanna was among the faithful disciples in the upper room after the death of Christ. (Acts 1:12-14) (Acts 1:14b)

CONCLUSION

People like Joanna, Mary Magdalene and their colleagues are still needed in the Church of the Lord Jesus Christ today. Serious spiritual ministry of the type the Lord Jesus Christ and His disciples exercised always requires full-time spiritual service. But when this occurs, who are those who can avail themselves to the Lord God to be used to provide the material needs of His servants? People like Joanna and her friends may never be seen in ministry in public but their ministry is purposeful and powerful.

ELIZABETH, MOTHER OF JOHN THE BAPTIST

1

Text: Luke 1:5-25; 57-58

Theme: Elizabeth's example of Faithfulness in walking with God

INTRODUCTION

Elizabeth is known in the Bible as the wife of Zechariah, the mother of John the Baptist and a relative of Mary the mother of Jesus. Her story offers us several character lessons some of which are going to be discussed in this sermon as follows:

DISCUSSION

I.   ELIZABETH LIVED AS ZECHARIAH'S FAITHFUL WIFE (Luke 1:5)

II. ELIZABETH LIVED AS A RIGHTEOUS AND SAINTLY WOMAN (Luke 1:6)

III. ELIZABETH AVAILED HERSELF TO BE USED FOR GOD'S GREAT WORK (Luke 1:57-58)

CONCLUSION

Whenever God uses somebody in the Bible to achieve a noble purpose, then it means that person has paid a certain price to make this possible. God always has a high and holy standard which has to be met by all His faithful people before He uses them. God could use Elizabeth to provide a forerunner for Jesus because Elizabeth paid the price for her to be used in this way as we have learnt in this sermon

Text: Genesis 22:14

Theme: Some precious lessons in the life of Elizabeth

INTRODUCTION

Looking at the way she lived for God and walked with Him, it is not possible to give a close scrutiny to the life of Elizabeth without learning several precious lessons as a Christian. This is exactly what we intend to do in this sermon. We want to look at some of the preeminent character traits in her life which are worth emulating. What are these prominent character traits? Some of them can be picked from her life as follows:

DISCUSSION

I. ELIZABETH'S LIFE PORTRAYS THAT GOD IS A PROVIDER
    1. God provided Elizabeth with a comforter in the visit of Mary. (Luke 1:41) (Genesis 22:14)

II. ELIZABETH'S LIFE TEACHES US THE IMPORTANCE OF SPIRITUAL PARTNERSHIP
    1. God sent Mary to Elizabeth for them to get mutual encouragement and edification in what He had planned to do with both of them. (Luke 1:39-41, 56) (1 Thessalonians 5:11)

III. ELIZABETH'S LIFE PROVES THAT GOD ALWAYS KEEPS HIS PROMISES
    1. The name Elizabeth means "God keeps his oaths." So her becoming pregnant in good old age proves that God always keeps his promises. (Luke 1:36) (2 Corinthians 1:20)

IV. ELIZABETH'S LIFE SHOWS THAT WE SHOULD ALWAYS CHECK OUR SPIRITUAL PRONOUNCEMENTS

1. We should always be full of grace as Christians and bless instead of cursing. (Luke 1:42) (Romans 12:14)
V. ELIZABETH SHOWS US THAT OUR FELLOWSHIP WITH OTHERS MUST ALWAYS LEAD THEM TO PRAISES
1. After Elizabeth had spoken well to Mary, she naturally burst into praises. (Luke 1:46-55) (Psalm 103:1-5)

CONCLUSION

This sermon has shown us that Elizabeth truly had excellent personal character traits worth emulating today. Saintly women were used in the Bible because they were true saints! By her actions, attitude and conduct, Elizabeth has truly shown us that she was a genuine saint who deserved to be the mother of John the Baptist. Where are the 'Elizabeths' in the Church of the Lord Jesus Christ today? Will you be one of them?

PHOEBE

1

Text: Romans 16:1-2

Theme: Practical lessons from the life of Sister Phoebe

INTODUCTION

Phoebe is mentioned only once in the New Testament in connection with the ministry of Apostle Paul. It is very likely that Paul the great Apostle sent her with a letter to Rome just as he also sent people like Titus and others with letters to some designated churches. Though she is only briefly mentioned in the scriptures, her life offers us some practical lessons which are of great relevance to the leadership and ministry of the Church. The name Phoebe means, "Radiant", "Bright" or "Shining" which makes her a shining star in the ministry of the Church which is dominated by men. Let us look at her life in this sermon as follows:

DISCUSSION

I. PHOEBE'S LIFE PROVES THAT THE EARLY CHURCH VALUED AND RECOGNIZED WOMEN.

1. It is strongly possible that Paul sent Phoebe to Rome to deliver his letter to the church there. This proves that Paul and the early church placed high value on Christian women. (Romans 16:1a)

II. PHOEBE'S LIFE PROVES THAT WOMEN CAN BE USED IN MATTERS OF SERVICE AND WORSHIP

1.   Phoebe is described as a deaconess. This is a designation and an office of service which can also be translated as minister or servant. (Romans 16:1b)

III. PHOEBE'S LIFE PROVES THAT WOMEN ARE PART OF GOD'S WORKMANSHIP

1.   Apostle Paul describes Phoebe as a sister in the Lord making her part of God's workmanship and great family in the Church. (Romans 16:2)

CONCLUSION

Phoebe's life proves that though God needs the men as servants in His Church, saintly women like Phoebe also have a great role to play in the ministry and service of the Lord Jesus Christ. Her life should be a source of great encouragement to all faithful women in the church of the Lord Jesus Christ who are desirous to be useful to Christ.

RHODA

1

Text: Acts 12:13-16

Theme: Rhoda, the rose of God

INTRODUCTION

The name Rhoda means "Rose" which makes her a young character with a sweet-smelling fragrance among the believers who had gathered in the house of Mary, the mother of John Mark to pray for the release of Apostle Peter from the grips of Herod. Though she was very young, her role in this story was very significant.

DISCUSSION

I. RHODA WAS A YOUNG BELIEVER
    1. It is commonly believed by most Bible expositors that Rhoda was about fifteen years old when Apostle Peter's miracle took place. (Acts 12:13)

II. RHODA WAS A YOUNG GIRL WHO BELIEVED
    1. Upon recognizing Apostle Peter's voice after His miraculous release by the Angel, Rhoda instead of opening the door for him rather run quickly to inform the other believers. She believed firmly that it was Apostle Peter and made an open declaration of this. (Acts 12:14)

III. RHODA WAS A YOUNG GIRL WHO WAS INSISTENT AND BOLD

1. When Rhoda told the believers about Peter's release, they were incredulous. When she insisted it was Peter, they rather said it was his spirit or angel. (Acts 12:15)

CONCLUSION

God sometimes uses young people in ways which are marvellous. In the Old Testament, He used David to kill Goliath. Again He used Shadrach, Meshach and Abednego to defeat great King Nebuchadnezzar. In this story, He used Rhoda, a young girl to announce the good news of the release of Apostle Peter. All these episodes prove that young people can be a great tool in the hands of the great God just like adults.

THE WIDOW AND HER WIDOW'S MITE

1

Text: Luke 21:1-4

Theme: Lessons from the Widow and her Widow's mite

INTRODUCTION

Though the name of the poor widow is not specifically mentioned in the gospels, her lessons on faithful and sacrificial giving have become a lasting monument in the Church of the Lord Jesus Christ. Whereas other biblical passages on giving teach us the principles of giving, her life teaches us the practise of giving. It is therefore important to mention this virtue as a challenge to all in giving. The challenges offered by her life on giving are as follows:

DISCUSSION

I. GOD SEES EVERY SACRIFICE WE PROVIDE

   1. God sees every sacrifice we make in giving. Christ was not standing by the widow but He saw everything she put into the offering box. (Luke 21:1-2)

II. THE AMOUNT WE SACRIFICE IS MORE IMPORTANT THAN THE AMOUNT PHYSICALLY PAID

1. Sacrificial giving is more pleasing in the sight of God than abundant giving which does not touch us in any significant way. (Luke 21:3, 4)

III. BIBLICAL GENEROSITY DEMANDS FULL TRUST IN GOD'S PROMISES

   1. If we can give sacrificially to please God, then we must give in full recognition of His promises of blessing upon faithful givers. (Luke 6:38; Acts 20:35; 2 Corinthians 9:6)

CONCLUSION

Having learnt these practical lessons on giving from the widow in this sermon, how should we henceforth regulate our giving in the church? Should it be just to win human applause or to win God's favour, approval and blessings? With what motive should we henceforth give? And with what faith and expectancy should we also give? May the good God guide us to give generously to His glory.

SUBJECT INDEX

A

H

I

J

K

R

S

T

V